William C. Strong

**Fruit Culture**

and the laying out and management of a country home

William C. Strong

**Fruit Culture**
*and the laying out and management of a country home*

ISBN/EAN: 9783337227142

Printed in Europe, USA, Canada, Australia, Japan

Cover: Foto ©Andreas Hilbeck / pixelio.de

More available books at **www.hansebooks.com**

# FRUIT CULTURE

AND

## THE LAYING OUT AND MANAGEMENT
## OF A COUNTRY HOME

BY

### W. C. STRONG

EX-PRESIDENT OF THE MASSACHUSETTS HORTICULTURAL SOCIETY,
AND VICE-PRESIDENT OF THE AMERICAN
POMOLOGICAL SOCIETY

BOSTON
HOUGHTON, MIFFLIN AND COMPANY
New York: 11 East Seventeenth Street
The Riverside Press, Cambridge
1885

# PREFACE.

OCCUPIED as I have been for the past thirty years in the cultivation and sale of fruit and ornamental trees and shrubs, it is but natural that I should receive numerous inquiries as to varieties, their selection, and their culture. There are many books to which reference might be made, some of which are of marked excellence. Downing's "Encyclopædia of Fruits" is an enduring monument to the memory of the late Charles Downing and his brother Andrew J. Downing, who initiated the work. Few men would be willing, had they the ability, to give such careful, patient, and exhaustive descriptions of every known variety of fruits, as may here be found portrayed with disinterested faithfulness. But this is a book for the professed horticulturist and orchardist. More practical treatises have been written by J. J. Thomas, P.

Barry, and others, designed rather for orchardists and nurserymen. Numerous works have
also been written upon special fruits, as for example, Pear Culture, Grape Culture, Small
Fruits, etc.

It is not the aim of this small volume to take
the place of any of these. It is hoped, however, that the directions here given will be found
so condensed and so simple that any cultivator
of ordinary intelligence may find it a guide, and
may work his way to complete success, so far as
it is attainable in our climate. No rigid rules
can be laid down, which will apply to every case.
The cultivator must exercise an intelligent judgment; stirring the soil, feeding, pruning, watering, showering as he may think will bring his
fruit to the highest standard. It has been my
endeavor to state the fundamental principles for
the culture of each species of fruit, without go-
ing into extended discussion of differing methods and theories. The intelligent amateur will
find the pleasure of experiments in reserve, as
an unfailing stimulus to his interest.

In the descriptions of the habits of insects,
I have found great aid in the admirable treatise

of William Saunders, and I would **refer others** to this recent publication on " Insects **injurious** to Fruits " **if** fuller information upon **this point is desired.**

It is evident that a popular handbook covering so much ground must be condensed almost to the degree of meagreness, and that everything like sentiment must be excluded. The book is submitted in the hope that it may prove helpful to the inexperienced. A further volume upon the culture of Ornamental Trees and Shrubs is in preparation, and may hereafter be published.

W. C. S.

Newton Highlands,
*April*, 1885.

# CONTENTS.

## CHAPTER I.

## CHAPTER II.

## CHAPTER III.

## CHAPTER IV.

## CHAPTER V.

## CHAPTER VI.

## CHAPTER VII.

## CHAPTER VIII.

## CHAPTER IX.

## CHAPTER X.

## CHAPTER XI.

## CHAPTER XII.

## CHAPTER XIII.

## CHAPTER XIV.

## CHAPTER XV.

## CHAPTER XVI.

# LIST OF ILLUSTRATIONS.

———◆———

# FRUIT CULTURE.

## CHAPTER I.

### RURAL HOMES.

IT seems natural that every man should to some extent be a tiller of the soil. In the pursuit of any profession or commercial occupation, it is uniformly found to be a most wholesome diversion and relief to become interested in the culture of land. This was the original assigned work, from which no man can wisely cut himself entirely free. There are influences which spring from this close intimacy with the world of Nature, unheeded it may be, yet powerful in counteracting the narrowing tendencies of an exclusively professional life. Would it not be the wise course for all men of business to locate their homes a little outside the limit of their trade or profession, and in a place where they would be diverted by an interested observation of the processes of Nature? It is not wise to

1

remove beyond the influences of social life. But with the modern facilities for rapid transit, it is surely an easy matter to reach open neighborhoods, where the advantages of good society may be combined with all the delights of country life. The influence upon children, who can have the free roaming of the fields, and, better yet, who have the care of their little garden, and who are being educated to habits of observation at the same time that they are building up a firm constitution, is a consideration never to be ignored. It would be unwise to burden one's self with an estate which required more care than could be given without interference with other duties. In such case, that which should be a relief and a tonic becomes a tax and a burden. It is far better to begin in a moderate way, extending as we gain experience, and leaving the finishing and perfecting of the place to be done in a ripe old age. Though this volume is especially designed as a guide in fruit culture, yet a few directions in the selection and treatment of a locality may not be considered out of place.

### CHOICE OF LOCALITY.

The situation for a rural home is not always left to our choice, but when this can be had, an

elevated position is, for many reasons, greatly to
be preferred. The advantage of wide extent of
prospect is obvious. Breadth of view is an effect which is appreciated by every one, and to
most persons it is an essential requisite to the
enjoyment of country life. But in order to obtain this it is not generally necessary to seek the
highest positions, which are often isolated, bleak,
and inaccessible. Vistas and more satisfying
pictures are usually obtained from gentle eleva-
tions, especially if near the margin of a lake, or
river. But of more importance than the advantage of prospect is the essential condition of good
drainage from the house. To this end it is well
if the crown of a rise can be obtained, so that
water shall flow in every direction from the
house. In this way the essential condition of
salubrious air in the cellar and around the buildings can be secured. Should it be necessary to
build upon a level plain, the house should be
placed so high that the cellar floor would be
nearly up to the level of the plain.

*Treatment.* — It is all-important that the
drainage from the house should be free and.
rapid, and also that the house be so well above
the general surface that the air will circulate
freely around it. Trees of dense foliage should
never be allowed to interfere with this essential

rule of health.  Openness and the free play of
air and sunshine are indispensable to the enjoyment of a home in the country.  In the construction of the house it will be true economy to
employ an architect, and, if the grounds are extensive, the advice of a landscape gardener may
be of value, in the adoption of a wise plan, in
developing the estate, and in the avoidance of
errors, at the outset.  A few general directions
are here given for those who have but little
land, and who prefer to improve it according to
their own plan.  The plan is of first importance.
Let it be drawn upon paper, with a definite purpose to arrange every part in harmony with some
general idea.  In all cases, whether the estate be
large or small, the effect of breadth and distance
is desirable, and hence it is well to set the house
as far back from the public street as may be
consistent with other plans for the estate.  This
will allow the largest extent of lawn in front of
the house, and in a position conspicuous from
the house as well as from the street.

*A Good Lawn.* — Professor Beal has well said
that this is the essential element about which the
other graces cluster.  A rich, clean turf is the
one feature necessary to every pleasant home, —
so fresh in its quiet repose as never to weary by
its sameness, so harmonious and pleasing in color

as to be the best possible ground for the display
of trees, shrubs, or beds of flowers. The green
sward should extend up to and around the house,
and, stretching down the undulating slopes of the
lawn, would give favorable points for groups of
shrubs and large trees in projecting masses.
The preparation of a permanent lawn is simple,
but somewhat expensive, as it is essential that
the work be thoroughly done at the commence-
ment. A deep, rich, retentive loam is most desirable, in order to preserve the vigor and
color of the grass during periods of protracted
drought. If the soil is originally light or sandy
it will be necessary to cart on a liberal supply of
strong clay loam, or retentive meadow soil, securing a depth of at least a foot of strong soil. It
is also desirable that the subsoil should be stirred
with the plough, or by trenching, in order to encourage the roots of the grass to strike down
deep for moisture, in the dry season. For a soil
of average richness, four cords of good stable
manure, spread and ploughed in, to an acre of
land will give sufficient fertility for the start. It
is not well to encourage too rank and coarse
growth, at the beginning. Surface dressings can
be applied from time to time, as may be required.
It is most important that the surface be made
fine and smooth by frequent harrowings, until

all inequalities are removed and the ground is thoroughly pulverized. August and early September are usually the best months of the year for sowing the seed, although early spring sowing will give time for the young grass to become established before hot and dry weather sets in.

The Agrostis species of seeds is the basis for all good lawns, of which Rhode Island Bent (*A. canina*) is best, and may be sown alone at the rate of three to four bushels per acre. Red Top (*A. vulgaris*) is also good, but not so fine. A mixture which gives excellent results is also recommended, as follows: three bushels of R. I. Bent, or of Red Top, and one bushel of Kentucky Blue Grass (*Poa pratensis*). If this is sown in August a pound of white clover seed may be sown and rolled in, early in the spring. The bright blossoms of the clover enliven the bed of green and produce a charming effect. But many prefer a uniform carpet of green, and rely upon the Bent alone. Four bushels would be too heavy seeding for grass lands for a crop, but it is none too much for a thick carpet for the lawn. After sowing, a slight brushing with light birch boughs and a firm and thorough rolling with a heavy roller will finish the work. Bear in mind that the firm pressure of the soil is not only essential to a smooth surface, but also that the even germinating of the seed and the vigor of the young plants is equally dependent upon this condition.

## THE APPROACH.

The construction of **the driveway and of walks** will of course precede the finishing of **the lawn.** It is a common remark that nothing contributes more to the beauty of an estate than perfect roads and walks. This is true, but to multiply **or** extend them beyond actual requirement is not only a useless **expense, but, worse** than **this, it** cuts the place into senseless patches, **and tends greatly** to diminish the effect of breadth, which **is so desirable.** Confine the expanse **of gravel within** the narrowest space consistent **with free** approach. Rectangular walks, bordered on either side by beds of flowers, belong **to the geometric** style of gardening of past generations. **But** this has given place, for the great majority of cases, to what is termed the natural style, which consists in curved walks and planting in beds and in groups, in appropriate places on the lawn. **In** many cases it is by no means desirable to **construct walks** to flower beds or other objects of **interest.** Often they are **far more** attractive **in** the naturalness **of their** grassy surroundings. Yet we would by no means disparage the effect of a fine avenue, or the loveliness of a walk winding around groups of shrubbery until lost in the deeper shade of larger trees.

As a general rule, the approach to the house should not be at right angles, but by a gradual curve, which will avoid the effect of stiffness and also will afford the most favorable view of the house. A private drive, not being subject to the heavy usage of teams, will not require to be as thoroughly constructed as the public streets. Still it is best to do all such permanent work well at the outset. The first step will be to remove all the loam and soft subsoil, possibly to the lawn or kitchen garden, for the purpose of deepening the soil, or else to the compost heap. The width of this excavation, for estates of moderate size, should be about ten feet, and should broaden at the barn into sufficient space for turning, or else for circling around a group of shrubbery at least twenty feet in diameter, which will afford room for carriages to wheel and at the same time conceal the extent of gravel. The depth of this trench will vary with different soils, from fifteen to twenty-four inches. Unless very soft and inclined to be wet, the first depth will be sufficient. A small tile drain laid two feet below the bottom of this trench will be much less expensive and more effective than a greater depth of trench. This will insure a dry foundation for the drive, and prevent any soft spots in the spring, when the frost is coming out. A covering of stones to the depth of ten inches or a foot is a sure and solid bed upon which to place from five to eight inches of sharp gravel, until the centre of the road is raised at least three inches above the original surface. The larger stones in the gravel will, of course, be raked to the bottom as the carting proceeds. Should the gravel prove to be sandy and not sufficiently binding, it will be necessary to procure a moderate surface dressing of clay-gravel, which will roll down smooth and hard and leave the road crowning at the centre about four inches higher than at the sides. With this nearly water-tight roof at the surface and the subsoil drain below, the maintenance of a perfect driveway will be a trifling expense from year to year. Walks are constructed on the same principle as driveways, only with less need of deep excavations and stone foundations. Generally, they should be four feet wide, in order that two persons abreast may enjoy the beauties of the place together.

Further directions in regard to ornamenting the estate would be out of place in a volume designed as a guide in fruit culture. The first object should be to provide trees which shall be in progress towards a supply of fruits for family use. The selection and planting of trees and shrubs for ornament may be an after-consideration.

# CHAPTER II.

## FRUITS.

An important element in the enjoyment of country life consists in the cultivation of the various fruits adapted to the climate. The adornment of the grounds with ornamental trees and flowers may be considered, by many, to be more important than products which involve care and constant watching, and which can be purchased at less cost, perhaps, than we can raise them. Yet the advice given by Gerarde, two hundred and fifty years ago, needs but slight modification in our day: "Forward, in the name of God, graffe, set, plant, and nourish up trees in every corner of your grounds, the labour is small, the cost is nothing, the commoditie is great, yourselves shall have plenty, the poore shall have somewhat in time of want to relieve their necessitie, and God shall reward your good mindes and diligence." Every one who engages in this occupation will testify to the strong and healthy interest awakened by the

processes of planting, nursing, and bringing to
successful maturity of the manifold fruits with
which this latitude is favored.    There are difficulties and dangers enough in the way to stimu-
late, but not to discourage, — to keep alive an
anxious interest which will add much to the zest
of an abundant harvest.   And beyond this, the
aim should be to make the quality of the home
products superior to that which can be obtained
at the markets.   Fruits freshly taken from the
trees or vines, with no injury from keeping or
from transportation, are much more appetizing
and health-giving than those which are usually
exposed for sale.    It should, therefore, be the
ambition of every owner of land to cultivate
fruits to some extent, without regard to the question of pecuniary profit.    And if an interest
becomes awakened sufficiently to induce a study
of the best methods, it will speedily become a
matter of surprise what an amount and what
variety of products can be obtained upon a limited space, when under highest culture.   It is
true economy to give this thorough and high
cultivation, as an assurance of a good degree of
success and an unfailing source of enjoyment.
Poor culture is sure to disappoint, while the art
of developing to perfection is, to a degree, entering into the beneficent work of the Creator.

Such employment is essentially elevating and purifying, and should be sought as a relief and an antidote against the selfish influences of commercial **pursuits.**

## LOCATION OF THE FRUIT GARDEN.

This must be determined **to a** great degree by the character of the estate. It is desirable that the front be kept open and free, for ornamental decoration. Fruits are consigned to the rear, generally **at** one side of **the** barn and out-buildings. **For convenience in working** and for mutual protection, **it** is desirable **to** concentrate the **various fruits in** one locality **so** far **as is practicable.** But it may be important **to** separate **the** peaches **and** grapes to a high, light, warm, and dry soil, and the pears, quinces, **and** plums to a heavier and retentive **loam.** Circumstances must determine the arrangement, **according** to the amount, the quality, the shape, and the aspect of the land.. As a general rule, apples should occupy the outer rank, as a defense and wind-break. Cherries are also strong and vigorous **in** growth, and being symmetrical **in form** may flank the **most conspicuous side.** Grapes **will want all the** sun **and air** that **can be** given. The same is true of the **peach,** the point to be obtained in each case being a moderate growth of thoroughly ripened wood, in order to insure hardiness. Raspberries, gooseberries, and currants may go between the rows of pears and other trees, and in partial shade. Dwarf pears and the quince will require the most retentive soil in the garden. By this it is not meant that water should ever stand, or that the ground should remain wet and sodden for a length of time after heavy rains. Such a condition is fatal to all garden fruits. Artificial drainage must be applied at the outset, if not provided by the nature of the soil.

Contrary to the prevailing impression, a comparatively elevated site is the safest position for all fruits which suffer from frosts. In the valleys the soil is richer in vegetable matter, the atmosphere is more humid, and evaporation from the foliage is less rapid. The result is that vegetation is more succulent and tender than that which is on higher ground. Add to this that the changes in temperature are much greater in valleys than upon hills, and the reason becomes plain why the peach is fruitful on high land, when it is killed in protected, low places. It is not only, or mainly, that the thermometer runs to the lowest extreme in the winter. But in the summer nights also, the cold air settles down into the valleys, causing a dank chill, which is in

marked contrast with the confined heat of mid-
day. Such violent changes are not conducive to
the healthy development of any fruits, and are
especially prejudicial to the peach and the grape.
The liability also to late spring and early fall
frosts is another serious objection to low lands.
Every one has noticed the marked line where
frosts have extended so far up a hill-side, leaving the foliage cut and withering below, while
above the line the verdure is as fresh as ever.
This sudden and premature check to the sap when
it is in full flow and before the wood is ripened
is a great injury to tender trees. It is, therefore,
desirable to select a site even beyond the proximity to frosty lands. An elevation tends greatly
towards the thorough ripening and hardening of
the wood of fruit trees. It is, therefore, not surprising that peaches, for example, are hardy and
fruitful on the hills as far north as the lower
counties in New Hampshire, while they seldom
do well in the southern part of New York.

But in advocating elevated localities, it is to
be remembered that they are exposed to bleak
and exhausting winds, which are liable not only
to shake the fruit from the trees, but, worse than
this, to cause excessive evaporation from the foliage and seriously to check growth. We well know
how vegetation is dwarfed as we ascend moun-

tains. We must avoid extremes. In the middle course there is safety. Much may be done in the way of protecting exposed sites by means of buildings, high fences, or, better still, by living wind-breaks. Experiments by the late Mr. Tudor prove that on the bleak promontory of Nahant the fierce blasts of the Atlantic may be so sifted, by high lattice, that trees will flourish, though they would quickly perish under full exposure. The Norway spruce is perhaps the best sheltering tree for all kinds of soil. American arbor vitæ is more compact and upright in growth, and is excellent in strong, retentive land. Austrian pine is most hardy for the bleakest positions. A belt of such trees planted from four to eight feet apart would have a sensible effect in modifying the asperity and also the degree of the cold.

### SUCCESS IN FRUIT CULTURE.

Taking into consideration the time and the labor involved in planting and in nursing, and adding the uncertainties and the fact of the constantly increasing liability to attacks from insects and diseases, it may seem that to the small cultivator fruits will cost more than they are worth. It is well to count the cost at the outset, because the difficulties are considerable, and eternal vigilance is the price of success. The list of

injurious insects is so long and formidable as to
be discouraging. Undoubtedly, the injury done
by vegetable and animal parasites far exceeds
the general apprehension. And the evil will
constantly increase unless held in check. The
codling moth is rendering many apple orchards
worthless. The curculio destroys all the plums,
if unmolested, and so infests the cherry that the
fruit in the market which is free from the immature larvæ is rather an exception. Mildew
is the scourge of the vineyard. The peach falls
a victim to " the yellows," and the pear to the.
" fire blight." Manifold are the difficulties, as
every cultivator can testify. But in these days
of inventive genius, when weapons of human
warfare are brought forward which are to mow
down whole armies at one discharge, or shake
cities to their foundations in the twinkling of an
eye, are we to acknowledge our inability to cope
with these minute insect enemies? The truth
is, we are gaining knowledge of the habits of
these enemies, and methods for their destruction, with great rapidity. There is now scarcely
a case where good culture and a vigorous application of remedies will not obtain the mastery.
The list of diseases seems long and formidable,
but, in practice, the surprise will be how readily
they yield to treatment. The difficulty is that

our gardens and orchards have been neglected,
the culture has been shiftless, and remedies have
not been applied, so that insects have largely increased in numbers. But most of them can
readily be reached by the powerful remedies
now at our command. Tobacco water and strong
soap-suds are effectual against most of the aphi-
dæ, the currant worm, and many other larvæ.
Petroleum, churned with soap or sour milk until
it will dilute with water, is a new remedy which
is likely to prove cheap and powerful. Arsenic
in the form of London-purple or Paris-green is
still more powerful, should it prove necessary to
bring such tremendous ordnance to bear upon
so minute a foe. With anything like a faithful
and persistent use, on the part of cultivators,
of weapons now at hand, we might hope for a
great reduction of these insect pests. The field
is full of encouragement to keep our trees and
plants in much cleaner condition than has been
prevalent in the past.

### PROFIT IN FRUIT CULTURE.

The strawberry yields the most speedy return,
and is generally regarded as the most remunerative. Under generous culture it will yield from
3,000 to 5,000 boxes per acre. Exceptional crops
of 8,000 boxes are reported. There should be a

good margin for profit, even with the smallest
number.

With proper care to keep the foliage of raspberries clean, and the canes vigorous, it is believed they would yield a larger and more permanent profit. They are a neglected fruit, but
deserve much better care. The sale of the better kinds must depend upon the local markets,
as they cannot be transported in good condition
for long distances. But they command a better
price than strawberries, and they require less
care in continuing the supply from year to year.
In the vicinity of good markets they hold out
strong inducements to the faithful cultivator.
The demand for currants and gooseberries is
more limited, but in the vicinity of cities they
are regarded as profitable by market gardeners.

The great drawback in the return of pears has
been that too many unsalable varieties have
been cultivated. The Bartlett and the Anjou
have been quite profitable and doubtless will so
continue to be. The danger now is that they
will become too abundant in their season, while
at other seasons there may be a lack. Seckel
and Sheldon may safely be planted for the market. The demand for winter pears is surprisingly
limited. But the Lawrence can be raised and
ripened almost as easily as an apple, and can be

sold at a good profit. With a soil and climate adapted to the production of the apple in its highest excellence, it is surely our own fault if we do not make it remunerative. The price is low and so is the cost. It should be our ambition to attain the minimum cost and maintain the highest quality. Most of us, however, are not in quest of so long an investment.

One year of success will cover the cost of two or three years of failure in the peach crop. North of New Jersey the risks are great. Where the soil and situation are right, many will venture and some will draw a prize. Cherries are difficult to pick, and are profitable only where pickers are plenty at a low rate. In respect to the grape, different localities must determine which varieties to plant for profit. Near some of the lakes of New York and on the shores of Lake Erie the Catawba and Isabella ripen well and are produced in large quantities, but they are useless in other sections, and varieties of inferior quality must take their place. The Concord is earlier and has been the leading market grape for a score of years past. Moore's Early and Worden are coming to the front, being of the same type, but earlier. Great confidence is expressed in the Niagara by those who have observed its hardiness and productive qualities.

The money standard is the test of success, doubtless, in fruit culture, as well as in all else; and fruits will endure this test as well as any products of the farm. Indeed, when we consider the special adaptation of the northern belt of States, in climate and soil, for the production of apples of superior quality, the vastly increasing demand for fruits of all kinds, which outruns even the rapid increase in population, and also the better methods of culture which are now known, we may safely say that the field is most encouraging, and that skill and patience, combined with enough capital for a fair start, will be sure of an abundant reward in an average of years. But beyond this, who can estimate the educating, refining, and elevating influence which comes from an intelligent following of this pursuit? It is an employment which never satiates, and which ever opens new doors for experiment and improvement. It is but fair that a considerable per cent. of credit be given for the wholesome influence which appertains to this calling.

# CHAPTER III.

IT is more economical to have fruit trees propagated in quantity, by those who make it their business, and who have facilities for their work. It is therefore customary for amateurs to supply their wants by purchasing from nurserymen. Where it is possible, it is better to select at some local nursery and transfer them, with no exposure of the roots and little delay in time, to their future home. Roots that are packed in wet moss and thus protected may be transported long distances without injury. It is possible also to restore roots that have been dried, by soaking in water for a day or two, and by syringing the tops for some time after planting. Yet it is far better to avoid the necessity of such expedients. For the apple, pear, plum, cherry, and quince, trees two or three years from the bud are to be preferred. Older trees can be moved with a good degree of certainty, and more speedy returns in fruit may thus be obtained. But there is less risk in the removal of small trees; they can be more easily handled, are not so much checked, and consequently more speedily recover from the shock of transplanting. In addition to these reasons, the best time to commence the formation of symmetrical heads is when they are young, about three years from the bud. The peach is an exception. Being very rapid in growth and forming fruit buds at once, it is desirable to select trees but one year from the bud. The subsequent directions given for pruning will indicate that older trees are objectionable.

*Quality.* — Clean, straight, and thrifty trees should be selected, such as have made vigorous growth the year previous. It is quite useless to mark the point of compass how the tree stood in the nursery, as this will not affect the new position in the slightest degree. It is, of course, important to obtain good sound roots and plenty of them. It is a mistake, however, to suppose that minute, fibrous roots on the apple, standard pear, and cherry are most desirable. Such as these are too frail to endure the process of transplanting. It is the roots which are of the size of a pipe-stem and upwards which have substance enough to bear the change, and vitality to throw out feeders at once. Good plantsmen often clean out all the fine, fibrous roots, when they have a supply of larger size, believing the first to be worse than useless, as likely to decay, and also as preventing the even packing of the soil among the roots. Many kinds of roots will endure hours of exposure to the air, or even to the sun, and to cold, drying winds, without being killed. But it is folly to permit results which are sure to follow such want of care. A feeble life is the worst that can befall a tree. Better that it should die outright than continue without making a good start the second year. In order to this it is necessary to keep the roots from the air, as well as from the sun, except for the brief time necessary in doing the work. Trees should not be transported in open wagons without having their roots covered and kept moist. They may stand in a damp cellar over night, if their roots are sprinkled, but it is better to "heel" them into the ground even for this short time. Trees may outlive a great deal of abuse, but it is wretched economy to create an enfeebled condition at the outset. The pleasure in orcharding depends entirely upon securing thrift and vigor.

*How to Plant.* — Rules for planting are simple. All bruised roots are to be cut away, and also the broken ends of the roots are to have a clean cut, with such a slant that when the tree stands in the hole the cut surface shall press on the surface of the soil and be entirely hidden from sight. The holes should be considerably larger than to allow of stretching the roots out straight in all directions. The subsoil should be spaded to the depth of a foot below the position of the tree. If this is very poor, good loam may be worked in with it, but it is not wise to put manure in the bottoms of the holes. The trees should stand at about the same depth that they grew previously, not burying the roots too deeply in the subsoil, but allowing them free course near the surface. If necessary, it is better to bring a slight mound around the trunk, rather than to sink the roots below the surface soil. The earth should be worked in and among the roots evenly and with great firmness, so that no air spaces shall be left, and the roots shall be all separated and in close contact with the soil. This is the test work, and it should be done slowly, with little soil at a time, worked in with the hands if necessary, and made firm with a packing mallet, or with the toe of the foot. The soil should be dry and friable when this work is done. It is a mistake to select a rainy day for planting, as it is impossible to do good work with muddy soil. After the planting is finished, nothing more will be required, in the fall of the year, except a surface mulch of litter to protect from frost. In the spring it is well to give one soaking with water upon finishing the planting, in order still more effectually to settle the soil around the roots. Yet judgment is to be used as to the amount. A cold, wet, stagnant condition of the roots is very injurious, preventing the formation of new rootlets at the critical time. Many a newly planted tree has been injured by continued and excessive watering.

### TIME TO PLANT.

The fall is a good time to plant all hardy trees, provided the work is done thoroughly, so that the trees will not be shaken by the winds, and the roots will remain compact in the soil. If planted early in autumn young rootlets will often form, even before winter sets in. There can be no doubt that a tree thus set will make a better start than if transplanted in the spring following.

Doubtless the practice of fall planting has been prejudiced by careless work, leaving cavities among the roots, and planting so loosely that tall shade trees, especially, are swayed by the winds, and the roots are more or less drawn and disturbed; thus not only losing all the advantage of time, but also causing a friction and exposure which often prove fatal. Newly set trees are, of course, less able to endure hardship, and it is true that they are sometimes injured by the cold of winter. This is certainly true of the peach. It may therefore be judged best to lessen risks by delaying planting until spring. Except in the case of evergreens (which, being always in leaf, require to be treated on a different principle), it is well to plant as early in the spring as we can find the soil dry and friable. It is not well to put the roots in cold, clammy earth, to be paralyzed by a long period of inaction. On the contrary, it is important to keep the soil open and warm, so as to induce root action as speedily as possible. Excessive moisture is decidedly prejudicial. Frequent light stirring of the surface will allow air and warmth to penetrate to the roots and promote quick action. After growth has fairly started and as hot and dry weather sets in, a light mulch of litter will serve to keep the ground moist and not overheated. Mulching among fruit trees should be done with judgment, depending much upon the character of the soil and the condition of the trees. Often a heavy and compact mulch is very injurious, especially upon heavy lands, tending to bring the roots to the surface and preventing the influence of air and sunlight upon the soil. The effect may seem favorable for one or more seasons, but it will soon be found that the roots are all on

the surface and everything is stagnant below.
On the other hand, a light mulch upon a light
soil does undoubted service in modifying the
heat and moisture at the roots.  Frequent stirring and keeping the surface light is Nature's
mulch, which, for the majority of lands, cannot
be improved.

### PREPARING THE LAND.

A thorough preparation of the land beforehand is important.  If springy, or in the least
inclined to be wet, it should be underdrained
with tiles, thereby not only relieving from an
excess of moisture, but also changing the character of the soil to that friable condition which
will induce capillary attraction, and thus secure
uniform humidity.

It will save much after labor if the land is
ploughed two or three times and the subsoil
plough is run in the furrows, thus obtaining a
depth which will prove a great encouragement to
the roots.  After this, a light run of the cultivator and the hoe will be all that will be required
to keep the land open and clean.  Neither weeds
nor grass should be allowed to grow in the fruit
garden, but potatoes and other vegetables may
be planted between the rows, especially when the
trees are small.

Many cultivators of the apple hold a different opinion in regard to allowing grass to grow in the orchard. It is said that the roots are kept cooler by the grass, and that winter fruit is more crisp and does not mature as early as in cultivated fields. Professor Maynard advocates planting rocky and bushy hill-sides with the apple, without even clearing or breaking up. He suggests making good holes and doing good work at planting and fertilizing, but clearing away the brush afterwards. In this way he believes many waste and rocky slopes may be converted into healthy and profitable orchards without ever feeling the plough. Such soils often are admirable for the apple, and there is no doubt this tree has vigor enough to make its way under this rough culture. Of course it is not to be neglected in respect to food, pruning, or treatment for diseases. It is not to be doubted that many unproductive hills might be turned into orchards at small expense, and that a good quality of fruit might thus be obtained. We do not want too vigorous and succulent growth for the apple, and do not therefore assign it to our richest lands, or give it constant culture. There is no doubt, however, that the largest and the premium fruit will come from trees that have grown in cultivated land. And there is encouragement to give clean culture wherever the land is suitable. But it remains an important question to decide by trial whether the many waste and rocky slopes may be profitably utilized by planting with apple trees, with no attempt at regularity, or purpose to cultivate with the plough.

## FERTILIZERS.

It is true economy to bring the land into good heart at the time of planting, as the work can be done at less expense than afterwards, and the benefits resulting will be immediate and permanent. If the spot has a fair quality of loam, an addition of stable manure at the rate of ten cords to the acre may be worked in at the last light ploughing. It is wasteful to bury it too deeply.

If a little care is exercised to prevent the manure from coming in immediate contact with the roots, no harm will result from spreading the freshest horse-manure broadcast upon the land. Dry earth is such a powerful absorbent that shrewd cultivators recognize the economy in using the manure at its full strength, which is before heating, or " rotting," as it is called.

Stable manure contains all the elements of plant-food, always and in all soils giving good results, and hence it is called a perfect fertilizer. But it does not follow that it is always a judicious

or economical application.  As a general rule,
when the plants are young and growth of
wood is desired, it is found that the large percentage of nitrogen which is supplied from animal excreta is advantageous.  But the percentage of potash and phosphates is altogether too
small when the plants come into fruit, while the
nitrogen is in excess.  Hence it is cheaper and
much better to supply the potash and phosphate
in some other form than from the stable.

Wood ashes, if they can be obtained at about
thirty cents per bushel, and if of really good
quality, are the cheapest and the easiest form
to apply potash..  But the supply of unleached
hard-wood ashes is limited, and an article of
good quality is difficult to be found.  Crude
potash of commerce is reliable and can easily
be obtained, but the difficulty here is in its application.  It is almost as hard as stone and the
process of breaking and dissolving in boiling
water is troublesome.  The liquid is exceed-
ingly caustic and may be utilized in turn in dissolving crushed bones at the rate of four to five
pounds to a pound of potash.  A good deal of
heat is evolved and ammonia will escape unless
absorbed by covering with dry peat, or loam.
In this way the potash and phosphate become
available without paying for the absorbents by

the pound, which is an important point when
they constitute a considerable part of the com-
pound. But this labor in compounding is not
inviting, and those who use but small quantities
will prefer to buy the manufactured article,
weighted with the absorbent. A more available and probably the cheapest form of potash
is obtained from the German mines, as a high
grade muriate of potash. This may be applied
directly at the rate of 300 to 500 pounds per
acre. The phosphate beds of South Carolina
and other large deposits are the great source of
supply to the manufacturers, but the material
is too difficult to be reduced to an available
condition by the amateur. We must rely upon
animal bones for our phosphates, and this usually
in the easiest form for use and immediate action,
when ground to a fine meal. In avoiding the
labor of preparation we must submit to the un-
pleasant consciousness that the meal may not be
strictly pure, and at all events the bone has been
so thoroughly steamed that it has lost everything
that was soluble before grinding. Yet it is
recommended as the best form in which we can
apply phosphates. It may be spread by itself,
or mixed with the muriate of potash and the
two applied together.

Professor Maynard of the Massachusetts Agricultural College has used a mixture in the following proportions for the past two or three years, 1,000 pounds pure bone meal, 300 pounds high grade muriate of potash. This amount he considers sufficient for an acre of land. The result of this application, he thinks, has been entirely satisfactory upon all kinds of fruits. But if the growth of wood should seem at any time to be inadequate to the tendency to fruit, an addition of ammonia in the form of guano or stable manure might be added. As the special fertilizers can be easily spread, this may be done after the trees are planted. And this supply should be continued from year to year, varying the amount of these three elements, potash, phosphoric acid, and nitrogen, according to the condition of the orchard.

### CUTTING BACK.

However much care may be used in digging, the roots are much reduced in transplanting trees. Nor, as has been stated, is it to be regretted that the small fibres at the extremities should be shortened. But it is important that a corresponding shortening of the limbs should preserve a balance in the tree. The mode of pruning is indicated in subsequent pages, under the head of the different fruits. In general, shortening-in the growth of the previous season

to the extent of two thirds will balance the root
pruning and prevent the tree from being swayed
by the wind. This shortening should be done
with care to preserve the symmetrical form of the
tree, and with due regard to future development.
It is a barbarous custom to chop off the entire
head, as is sometimes seen. And yet it is advisable to cut back heroically as the best means of
inducing a strong and vigorous start. There
will also be much less occasion to use stakes for
the purpose of holding the trees firm while the
roots are taking hold. A little swaying is very
prejudicial to the formation of new roots.

### DISTANCES FOR PLANTING.

As a rule, fruit gardens are liable to be
crowded and too much shaded. There should
be sufficient space for the sun and air to penetrate and warm the soil. On the other hand,
trees are fond of society; they afford mutual
protection from high winds and scorching suns;
they preserve a gentle humidity in the ground
underneath, and therefore they should be planted
near enough for mutual support. Many varieties of the same fruit are much more vigorous in
growth than others, and all kinds are affected
by the quality of the soil, and hence allowances
are to be made.

The following table will serve as a general guide : —

| | |
|---|---|
| Standard Apples . . . . . . . . | 33 to 40 feet apart |
| Standard Apples, close pruned . . . | 25 " " |
| Dwarfs on Doucain stock . . . . | 10 " " |
| Dwarfs on Paradise stock . . . . | 8 " " |
| Standard Pears . . . . . . . . | 15 to 25 " " |
| Dwarfs on Quince . . . . . . . | 10 to 12 " " |
| Standard Cherries . . . . . . . | 20 " " |
| Dwarfs and Morellos . . . . . . | 10 to 15 " " |
| Peaches and Plums . . . . . . . | 12 to 15 " " |
| Quinces and Grapes . . . . . . | 6 to 8 " " |
| Currants and Gooseberries . . . . | 4 " " |

Raspberries in rows four feet apart and three feet in the rows.

Blackberries three feet in the rows, but a second row should be eight feet distant.

As an acre contains 43,560 square feet, it follows that it will accommodate about the number of trees shown in the table here given, depending somewhat upon the shape of the land.

| | | | |
|---|---|---|---|
| At 40 feet | 27 trees | At 12 feet | 302 trees |
| At 33 feet | 40 " | At 10 feet | 435 " |
| At 25 feet | 69 " | At 8 feet | 680 " |
| At 20 feet | 108 " | At 6 feet | 1208 " |
| At 15 feet | 193 " | At 4 feet | 2720 " |

# CHAPTER IV.

THERE is no exception to the rule that fruit trees thrive best in soil that is kept loose and free from all weeds and grasses. Cherries will do better than most other fruits in grass land, and they may thereby be kept from too luxuriant growth. But even these, when in bearing condition, will scarcely endure this check. For all other fruits it is far better to keep the ground lightly stirred with the cultivator and hoe. The finely pulverized condition of the surface is a great help in the aeration of the soil, giving warmth and vigorous action to the roots. But it is important to guard against deep ploughing among the roots, thus disturbing the small fibres which are in quest of food. It is not wise to draw these fibres too near the surface by a heavy mulch, lest they perish when the mulch decays or is removed. On the other hand, we must guard against driving the roots into the subsoil by injuring the surface feeders.

Two or three inches in depth of floury earth is the best mulch we can provide. Beyond the ordinary implements of the garden a hand-engine or forcing-pump will be essential for the purpose of syringing and applying the various remedies against insects. Some light pattern which draws from a pail, like the Johnson patent, is most convenient. The Waters pruning pole is also indispensable, doing the work of pruning with great ease. If this is attended to at the proper time there will be little occasion to use the saw.

### IRRIGATION.

Notwithstanding the boasted power of human skill and energy, the works of man are so feeble in comparison with the mighty forces of nature, that it seems almost useless to attempt watering during a time of drought. During the season of active vegetation and evaporation most soils in our climate would be benefited by an inch of rain-fall in every five days, or six inches in a month. This involves 27,000 gallons, or 108 tons, of water to an acre, every five days. As the amount of rain often falls below one inch and seldom exceeds three inches per month, it is an important question whether we can undertake to supply such an enormous quantity to make up the deficiency. In the older States there are few streams which can be diverted and relied upon in a dry time to give a full supply. If access to streams or ponds of sufficient size can be had, it would doubtless be a wise investment for the enterprising fruit-grower to put in a wind-mill or a steam-pump, and a system of pipes. With steam the water may be forced directly from the pump, but with a wind-mill, a reservoir of large capacity, elevated from twenty to thirty feet above the field, would be necessary. It would thus be practicable to give an inch of water to an entire acre in a day, by using a hose one and a half inches in diameter, with a pressure of thirty feet head. The water should not be allowed to fall or run in a stream, thus supersaturating some parts and causing the ground to cake, but should be distributed in spray, like rain. To most cultivators it will seem to involve too much expense and labor to irrigate so extensively. Yet in many cases it would doubtless prove remunerative, especially for strawberries, which constantly cry out for water, water, water, — and again a little more water.

Will it be advisable to attempt to supply water in more limited quantities? It is said that it does more harm than good to partially water plants in a time of drought. It is true that when the soil is parched it sucks up a small supply as though it were nothing, so that the roots are rather tantalized than refreshed. If the same amount of water had been sprinkled over the foliage like a dew, at nightfall, the result would have been different. It is often quite beyond our power to give a sufficient quantity of water to reach the roots. But a much smaller quantity showered upon the leaves at evening will cool the air and greatly invigorate the wilting foliage. It is well known what beneficial results follow from heavy dews, though the amount of precipitation is very small. Every gardener understands the surprising benefit to foliage which is caused by a light showering in the greenhouse. Of course we cannot expect such luxuriant growth as comes from the confined humidity of the house. But it is reasonable to look for decided benefit to all kinds of fruits, even from a light sprinkling of the foliage at night. A force-pump upon wheels, or even a hand-engine, will do good service where the garden is small. A light sprinkling upon every clear night, especially in the early part of the season, will greatly increase the probability of obtaining the first prize.

### APPLICATION OF FERTILIZERS.

At what season shall we apply manures? It is evident that the roots take in nourishment during the summer, in the season of active growth. The application of liquid fertilizers at periods when fruit is growing has shown immediate and remarkable results, increasing the size, in marked contrast with that which received no liquid. It would seem that stable manures and many other fertilizers are leached or dissolved by heavy rains and speedily affect the roots. This is desirable only during the season of growth. When the roots are dormant it may prove a positive injury. A heavy dressing of fresh horse manure applied on the surface of a rose border in November seriously injured the roots. A similar experiment with liquid from horse manure, applied before the roses had commenced growth, proved equally injurious. But liquid of the same strength was freely used when the growth was vigorous, and with marked advantage.

The time of application must depend, to a considerable degree, upon the nature of the fertilizer. If easily soluble it can be used from time to time a little in advance of the requirements of the plant. If, on the other hand, it is slow in decomposition it should be applied either in the

fall or early spring. There can be no doubt
that horse manure rapidly loses in value if remaining in a heap. "Well-rotted manure" is a
term which signifies a product containing possibly not twenty-five per cent. of the original elements of plant nourishment. It is true it is reduced to a condition when it may be applied
freely to the roots and at once be taken up, but
the loss in strength has been enormous. Much
less loss will occur if the fresh manure is spread
broadcast and exposed to the sun and air. In
the last case considerable ammonia is undoubtedly set free, but there is no fermentation, and
the absorbing power of the soil and the effect
of the rains will carry a large percentage of the
value into the earth. As stable manure is slow
in decomposing, when not heated, it should be
applied early, but not in such quantity in the
fall that its strong juices shall penetrate to the
roots and burn them. A mulch of an inch or
so in depth will not injure the roots of apples,
pears, and quinces, and will protect them from
the winter frosts.

Spreading broadcast in the early spring and
working in with a sharp-toothed cultivator, as
fresh as can be got, is the most economical way
to use stable manure. It is a common opinion
that frequent turnings will prevent excessive

heating, and will reduce the manure to a fine, rotten condition. But every turning gives a fresh opportunity for the air to penetrate and the ammonia to escape, until so little is left that fermentation ceases. A much better way is to compost the stable manure with an equal, or a double amount of loam. This amount of loam will absorb the gases, and there will be little loss. The compost can be used freely without danger of injury, but a great deal of labor is involved in collecting, manipulating, and applying the compost. Experienced cultivators are now adopting the plan of conveying the manure as speedily as possible from the horse to the soil. If the quantity is not too large it will not injure the roots of trees. There is little danger of this when the roots are active. Cow manure is a cooler and safer material and may be used in large quantities at any season. More will be required than of horse manure. In making application of fertilizers it is to be remembered that the roots are not confined to a narrow circle around the trunk. Most of the feeding roots are roaming at a distance in search of nourishment. The height and size of the top will indicate in some degree how far the fertilizers should be spread.

Commercial fertilizers, so-called, embrace all

the various chemical elements and compounds of the market, including wood ashes, in distinction from stable manure, and its combinations with organic matter. In theory it would seem that the specific food of plants can be furnished in small bulk and at less cost, if labor is included, than we can apply the coarse products of the stable. That such food can be so supplied in concentrated form and with perfect results is beyond question. The simple point is, which is most available. This includes the question of first cost and the labor of applying.

Take the formula in use for all fruits on the grounds of the Massachusetts Agricultural College.

1,000 lbs. of fine ground bone would cost about **$25**
300 lbs. of high grade Muriate of Potash
(German Salts) . . . . . . . . . 8
                                  ———
                                  **$33**

This is supposed to be the average cost of a sufficient quantity to fertilize an acre. At least double this amount would be used by market gardeners, and probably an addition of nitrogenous matter, perhaps in the form of 500 pounds of fish guano. That the preparation is excellent and a perfect food, as it stands, is the testimony of cultivators, as well as men of science. The amount given about equals, in nutritive value, eight cords of stable manure of average quality. The average cost of stable manure, in the vicinity of large cities, is $8 per cord delivered on the farm. In some sections it is higher, and in others it cannot be purchased. But in the case supposed the cost per acre will be $64, in comparison with $33 for the bone and potash. That the latter preparation is better adapted to fruits, especially to peaches, grapes, and plums, there is little doubt. In the case of strawberries the mechanical effect of stable manure in retaining moisture is to be considered.

It is also to be remembered that the effect of stable manure is more lasting than that of chemicals, the land being benefited for two or three years after the application. On the other hand, chemicals are free from the seeds of weeds ; they are easily procured and applied as needed, and the potash has an undoubted tendency to check the white grub and perhaps other insects. The various brands of superphosphates are, as a matter of course, sold at a profit to the dealers, and it is difficult to make an estimate of their relative value. The analysis of the state inspector ought to be a guide, and if one is willing to pay liberally for the process of manipulating and mixing, he will buy the manufactured article from some dealer who has a reputation to sustain.

### THINNING THE FRUIT.

The design of nature is to produce the largest number of seeds, irrespective of the fruit. Hence the abnormal development of pulp is likely to overtax the ability of the tree to carry. The enormous crops of the Baldwin apple in one season so weaken the tree that it is unfruitful in the season following. It is a great evil to allow such excessive loads upon our trees. Even in cases where the amount does not seem to be more than the tree can support, it will usually be found that a reduction of one half, or more, will still result in a larger measure of fruit, by reason of the increased size of the remainder. And of course the quality and appearance is greatly improved. In addition to this all-sufficient reason, a still more weighty reason may be given. Just after the setting of the fruit the attacks of the codling moth, the apple maggot, the curculio, and other insects commence. A careful inspection will reveal which fruits have been punctured. Such fruits are not only worthless, but they are also the hiding-places of the parents of a numerous progeny. It is therefore the best time to destroy these injurious insects. And let the work be done unsparingly

for the apple, the pear, and the peach. When
the fruit is small it will seem that none too many
specimens have set. With that seeming, it is
yet probable that from one half to three quarters
of these should be picked, including, of course,
the diseased and deformed specimens. The
largely increased size of the remainder will keep
the bulk about the same as if no reduction had
been made. Many instances indicate that the
bearing year of the Baldwin may be changed by
systematic picking. There can be no doubt that
more regular crops can be obtained by this
means. The labor involved is by no means as
great as would be anticipated. When the fruit
is so small it can be nipped off with great rapidity, and a surprising space gone over in a day.
In no way can time be more profitably spent in
the garden.

### LABELS.

What is in a name? A pear is a pear " for
a' that." True, but its real merit may remain
undiscovered, if its sign or lineage is unknown.
With some fruits it is necessary to know their
time of ripening and their habits, in order to
develop them to perfection. Then we want a
personal acquaintance with each individual, by
its name, if we would appreciate its good
traits to the full. In order to this, it will be

necessary to enter in a book the names of all the varieties of fruits in the order of their planting. And, besides this, and that we may promote a familiar observation of all the characteristics of each variety, its form, color, vigor, and varying habits, it will be necessary to supplant the wood labels of the nurseryman by something more permanent, which shall be attached to each specimen or at least so accessible that he who runs may read.

Painted stakes, written upon with a lead pencil before the paint is hard, or with a lamp-black brush, are often used for labeling the small fruits. Strips of sheet zinc about half an inch wide, and tapering to a slender point at one end, are easily twisted loosely to a limb, and are permanent and accessible without being too conspicuous. The surface of the zinc being first allowed to oxidize in the open air, and then moistened, may be written upon with a common lead pencil, and the marking will remain legible for a score of years. For small fruits these zinc strips might be attached to iron pins. This is a neat, cheap, permanent, and very satisfactory mode of marking.

# CHAPTER V.

BEYOND question this is the most important fruit of our latitude. The abundance, cheapness, and certainty with which the apple can be raised are important points in its favor. The price of this fruit is sometimes so low, in years of abundance, that farmers are inclined to say it does not pay to raise it. Yet the cost of producing is so little that probably no New England farm crop pays a better interest, in an average of years. There are thousands of loamy hill-sides, with fair natural drainage, where land is held at farm prices, which invite to a long, it may be, but certainly to a safe and permanent investment in apple orcharding. Our climate and our soil are right for producing the highest quality. We are near to local markets and to the seaboard. The fruit is wanted in almost unlimited quantity; it can be kept and transported for long distances, and the labor in cultivating, harvesting, and marketing is divided over so long time that the work is done without hurry or risk. When we add to these considerations the intrinsic value of the apple for domestic purposes, and of its juice for vinegar or for boiling to a syrup for culinary use, we must readily admit that it easily takes the front rank. Yet it does not follow that it is to be planted freely upon country places of limited extent. The various insects which injure the fruit are more readily destroyed in an orchard, by systematic attention, than upon a few scattering trees. Moreover, the price of the fruit is usually low, the trees are spreading and require space. Our land may be too valuable and precious to allow them more than the corners or an odd angle. But the best early and autumn varieties we must have for our own family supply, and if our space will not admit the winter kinds, we can rest assured the market will be well supplied with such at moderate cost. With such moderate wants we shall be troubled in selecting from so many hundred candidates. We will make an extremely limited list.

*Early Harvest.* — One of the earliest; bright straw color, mild' acid, oblate, stock rather short and slender, flesh nearly white, quality fine, but liable to be wormy; few perfect specimens. July and August.

*Early Sweet Bough.* — Large, oblong-ovate,

4

greenish-yellow; flesh tender, sprightly, rich, sweet; productive, excellent. Ripens in August.

*Red Astrachan.* — A Russian variety. Large, roundish, nearly covered with deep crimson and a beautiful bloom; flesh tender, juicy, rich, acid. July and August.

*Williams' Favorite.* — Large, oblong-ovate, smooth, mostly fine dark crimson; flesh yellowish-white, moderately juicy, pleasant. Its fine appearance adds to its reputation.

From these four summer kinds, perhaps the first choice for family use would be Sweet Bough, the second would be Astrachan, and the third, Williams. Either one of these will do, and a single tree, if vigorous, will give an ample supply of this transient early fruit for one family. American Summer Pearmain, Benoni, Early Joe, Early Strawberry, High Top Sweet, Primate, and Summer Rose are all good early kinds, if variety is desired. The amateur may graft them on different limbs of the same tree for the purpose of experiment, and thus avoid the burden of an excessive supply.

*Gravenstein.* — This is, par excellence, the variety for the autumn months. Fruit large, roundish, slightly ribbed; yellow, striped and splashed with bright red; flesh tender, juicy, sub-acid, very rich and high flavored; very productive, handsome, and excellent. Still another merit may be added, that its period of ripening extends over the entire fall months. With so many good qualities combined in one, the market-man will not add other kinds, and the amateur may well be content with this.

*Porter.* — An old favorite; fruit large, oblong-conical; bright yellow; flesh tender, rich, rather acid; fair and productive.

Other fall varieties may be named in the order of their merit as follows: Fall Pippin, Garden Royal, Jewett's Red (or Nodhead), Fameuse (or Snow), Jersey Sweet, Lyscom, and Maiden's Blush.

*The Siberian Crab,* belonging to a distinct species (*Pyrus baccata* and not *Pyrus malus*), also ripens in the fall. A single tree will be sufficient for jellies and marmalade. As an ornamental tree it is also quite effective, both in blossom and when loaded with its brilliantly colored fruit. Among the best are Transcendent, Montreal Beauty, and Lady Elgin.

It may be bewildering to make a selection from the long list of winter kinds, but the prevailing rule for a hundred trees for the orchardist (99 of Baldwin and 1 of — Baldwin) may assist in the decision. This universally known

variety has unquestionably more points of merit
than any other, and is so far in advance that the
foregoing rule will apply to many sections, for
market purposes. Yet other kinds are superior
to it in quality, and its tendency to overbear and
exhaust itself to barrenness, in the odd year,
creates such a fluctuation in the quantity of the
crop and in the price, that it is specially desirable to have more uniformly productive kinds, and
of higher quality.

*Esopus Spitzenberg.*—This variety is scarcely
equaled in rich and high flavor; fruit round,
slightly conical; color high, rich red, faintly
striped; flesh yellow, firm, crisp, spicy, brisk acid,
superior; moderately productive. In some sections it is shy in fruiting, but where it flourishes
it will rank as best.

*Northern Spy.* — Large, roundish conical;
pale yellow, slightly striped with dark red; flesh
white, tender, fine, sprightly sub-acid, aromatic;
beautiful and of best quality. Does not bear
when young and requires good culture, which it
will well repay.

*Hubbardston Nonesuch.* — Large, round-
ovate; color rich yellow, striped and dotted
deep red; flesh yellowish, very rich, sub-acid,
excellent flavor; early winter.

*Rhode Island Greening.*—Large, roundish

oblate; green or greenish-yellow; flesh yellow, tender, juicy, rather acid; very productive, single trees sometimes producing forty bushels of uniform fruit.

*Roxbury Russet.* — Medium; rough russet or greenish color; flesh crisp, good, sub-acid flavor. Keeps until spring.

*Tallman's Sweeting.* — Flesh firm, rich, very sweet. Excellent for baking.

Other excellent winter kinds are Canada Renette, Cogswell, Jonathan, Lady, Mother, and Peck's Pleasant. Numerous other kinds exist which may have slight shades in flavor, or qualities, which entitle them to enter the ranks in large collections, and possibly by good behavior to advance to the front. Occasionally a seedling attains a permanent reputation. But it is rather surprising how few of our best apples are of recent origin. We may safely plant the standard kinds, in confidence that they will not be speedily superseded.

Apple trees should be planted at least thirty-three feet, and better than this, forty feet apart for permanent orchards, in the latter case giving forty-nine trees to the acre, the outside rows being fifteen feet distant from the outer line. But for family purposes it is generally found best to plant these near the outer line of the estate, or in corners which will allow single specimens. It is a prevailing impression that the fruit of branches which overhang a neighbor's land belongs to him. But this is a mistake; he has a right to remove the limbs, but the fruit is yours, though it is doubtful if you have a right to enter his land for the purpose of picking. If the tree stands upon the line, the rights of course are mutual, and neither party can injure the tree without consent. Your neighbor cannot complain of shade, or dampness from trees upon your land, however near they may be to the line, but he may cut the roots which penetrate his land. It is unnecessary to add, that a purpose to insist upon legal rights among neighbors will bear only fruits of bitterness.

Apple trees are supposed to need little care after planting, and therefore are frequently left to receive only an annual scraping and pruning in March. This is the reason why so large a proportion of our orchards are in such a stunted condition. No tree better repays generous culture. It will better endure a grass sward than the pear, but this should not be allowed to be thick or exhausting. An annual surface dressing of stable manure, in November, say half of a one horse-load to each tree of full size, will keep it in permanent vigor. Pruning of all suckers and of

crowding limbs should be done in June and
July, but a heavy removal of foliage at this season will cause stunted growth. Should it be
necessary to remove heavy limbs (an evil to be
avoided by summer pinching and pruning, as
far as possible), this may be done in March,
care being taken to smooth the cut even with
the trunk, and painting it with shellac dissolved
in alcohol or with grafting wax. The wound
thus covered will not heal as rapidly as if made
in June, but, on the other hand, the check to the
tree is much less if the pruning is done while
the buds are dormant. The usual practice of
severe scraping in the spring is unnatural and is
often injurious. Obviously it is well, after the
severity of winter is past, to give the trees a good
rubbing, and thus remove the rough bark and
moss which serve as a harbor for insects. But
scraping down to the quick and exposing to the
cold and evaporation of March winds must result in injury. The practice of giving a heavy
wash of caustic lime, after scraping, is also to
be condemned. A moderately strong wash of
potash water will assist in cleansing the trunk
and large branches and in giving a bright green
and healthy appearance to the bark; but under
generous culture this will seldom be found necessary.

The fruit for winter use should remain on the trees until danger of sharp frosts, and then be hand-picked and placed in clean barrels, with greatest care not to bruise. Every imperfect specimen should be rejected. The picking should be done in a dry day, and the barrels should remain open a few days to allow for "sweating." Afterwards the barrels should be headed and placed on their sides in a cold store-room, or on the north side of a building, until in danger of freezing, which is usually in the latter part of November in New England. The barrels should then go to a cold and moist cellar. In a warm and dry cellar the fruit shrivels and matures prematurely. At a moist temperature of 32°, Roxbury Russets keep an infinite time.

Cider made from sound fruit, and allowed to work only to the point of clarifying, is a healthful and a temperance beverage. It is not to be made after the manner of the farmers of old from all sorts of fruit, rotten and wormy, or otherwise, and then encouraged to ferment until it becomes "hard," but with a family mill, costing from twelve to twenty dollars, a grinding of a bushel, or a barrel, of fruit from time to time will give a fresh supply of a mild, agreeable, and innocent drink.

Apple juice boiled down to one quarter of its

bulk becomes a thick syrup, which will keep indefinitely, and is useful for flavoring and moistening mince pies, for sauces, and various cooking purposes.

*Dwarf Apple trees* are obtained by grafting upon the Paradise and the Doucain stock. The former is the most dwarfed, being little more than a bush, and throwing the tree into fruit in two or three years from the graft. The Doucain is intermediate, and will produce small trees which will last many years. It is well adapted for garden culture, giving the advantage of early fruitfulness, an increase in the number of small trees, and consequently in the number of varieties, when this is desired. But it is obvious that strong growing roots will sustain large tops and yield the best results, in extensive culture. Paradise Dwarfs may be planted eight feet apart, Doucain ten feet apart. Constant watchfulness will be required in the culture of dwarfs to give annual supplies of food, to preserve the form by pruning, and also to prevent rooting above the dwarf stock and thus destroying its character.

### INSECTS INJURIOUS TO THE APPLE.

The Codling Moth, or apple worm (*Carpocapsa pomonella*). This insect was imported from Europe early in the present century, and

because of its rapid spread over the entire con-
tinent, the difficulty of exterminating, and the
extent of damage which it does, it has become
the most serious evil which the orchardist has to
meet.    The moth appears at the time of flower-
ing, depositing its eggs singly in the calyx end
of the young fruit, as it is forming.   The egg
hatches in a few days, and the worm bores to the
heart of the fruit, and from thence works its
way out at one side, a full-grown flesh or pink-
ish-colored worm, in three or four weeks from
the egg.   It then enters into the cocoon state,
finding shelter about the trunk of the tree, and
in two or three weeks more is transformed into
a moth for the second generation.   The second
crop of larvæ, if they escape from the fruit before it is gathered, spin their cocoons under the
loose bark of the tree, or some similar shelter.
But if carried with the fruit to the cellar, they
will be found around the crevices and hoops of
the barrels.

Figure 1 is copied from Saunders's work upon
insects, as best illustrating the habits of this
most destructive pest.   The puncture by the
moth is represented at *b*, the borings of the
larva at *a*, the mature worm at *c*, the moth with
wings closed at *f*, the moth with wings ex-
panded at *g*, and the cocoon at *i*.

*Remedies.* — The castings of the worm in June usually adhere to the young apple at the calyx. If all the diseased fruit could be picked and destroyed before the worm leaves the fruit, the remedy would be effectual. Gathering this fruit after its premature fall is useless vigilance,

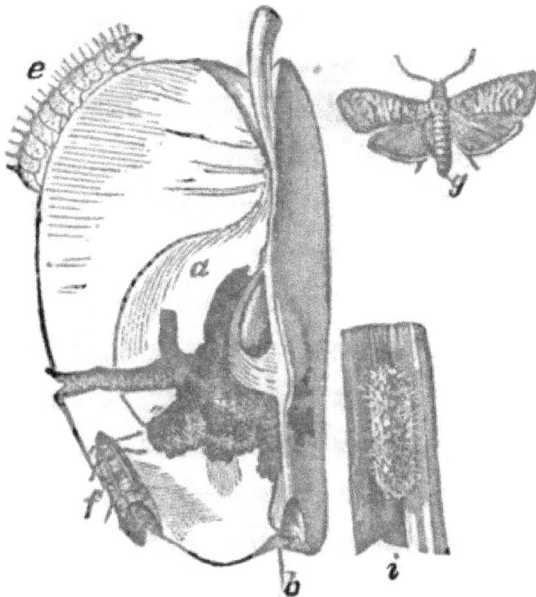

Fig. I.

after the rogue has left. Cloth bandages tied around the trees early in June will serve as traps where the cocoons will collect. These should be examined two or three times in July and August and the cocoons destroyed. Cleaning the limbs and trunks of the trees and also the fruit barrels and the fruit cellar, in early spring, may also destroy many cocoons. Fruit which has been attacked falls prematurely, but usually not until the worm has left. This is not always so, and therefore this fallen fruit should always be gathered. The moth is not attracted by light, and hence cannot be caught to any extent in this way. A more effectual remedy, as is claimed by many Western orchardists, is the use of London-purple and Paris-green, syringing the trees at the time the fruit is first forming, in a similar way to that hereafter described for the canker-worm. It is earnestly to be hoped that cautious experiments will indicate that this most destructive pest may thus be controlled.

The Apple Maggot is a footless, greenish-white grub, one fifth of an inch long, with a pointed head, but cut squarely off behind. It frequently attacks apples that have been previously perforated by the codling moth. It is also frequently very injurious to the fall varieties and those having thin skins; and it is sometimes found working in the winter fruit, doing serious damage. No effectual remedy has been discovered.

The Tent Caterpillar (*Clisiocampa Americana*). This is a prevalent and conspicuous enemy, but one easily met and destroyed. The moth deposits its nest of 200 to 300 eggs in July, near the ends of small branches, encircling them as seen in Fig. 2. The eggs, being covered with a gummy water-proof varnish, remain until the opening of leaf-buds in the following spring. After hatching, the young caterpillars rapidly increase in size, attaining to nearly two inches in length in the course of five or six weeks, when they are very voracious, often stripping large limbs of every vestige of foliage. The best time to destroy this insect is in March, before the nest-eggs are hatched. A careful inspection of the ends of the limbs will reveal most of them. If any should escape notice, the young colony can easily be detected and destroyed soon after hatching. It is sheer neglect, for which there is no excuse, to allow the worms to increase to full size. The tenting habit of the worm makes it a trifling task to destroy it, when it is small. As it in-

Fig. 2.

creases in size, the tents become very unsighty, and the labor in crushing such a mass of vitality is much more troublesome. The wild-cherry is especially liable to be infested with this caterpillar.

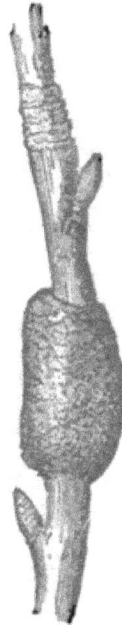

The Forest Tent Caterpillar (*Clisiocampa sylvatica*). This is a common pest at the West and South, being not only very destructive to the apple, but also feeding upon the oak, ash, and various other forest trees. In habit and form it closely resembles the common caterpillar, being, however, more active and migratory, marching rapidly in single column in search of food. Their egg nests may be easily distinguished by being cut squarely off at each end, as in Fig. 3. These egg clusters are to be sought and destroyed before the starting of buds. The young worms are not as easily detected as the common tent worm, but are to be sought early in the morning and in their early stages, before their migrations commence. They may

Fig. 3. then be easily destroyed.

The Round-Headed Borer (*Saperda candida*). This is a widespread enemy, preferring the apple, but common to the quince, mountain ash, and many other trees. The brown-colored beetle, with two broad, creamy white stripes running the length of his body, is about three fourths of an inch long; flying at night, and depositing its eggs singly in June and July under the loose scales of bark, near the surface of the ground. The worm soon hatches and penetrates to the sap-wood, excavating flat cavities of the size of a silver dollar in the inner bark, which are filled with sawdust-like castings. It is now supposed that the grub remains in these cavities for two seasons, often doing great and perhaps fatal injury to the tree, by completely girdling it under the bark. With the third summer the grub attains its maturity, aud towards its close its jaws have become strong enough to cut a cylindrical passage three or more inches into the solid wood, thence curving upward and outward to the bark, but without cutting it. This cavity is the home of the pupa the following winter, from which the beetle cuts a smooth round hole, and emerges nearly three years after the eggs were first laid. The deposit of eggs may be prevented by keeping the bark perfectly clean around the trunk, and by applying a coat of soft soap and washing-soda early in June and again in July. A mound of ashes, or air-slacked lime, placed around the tree in May will also deter the beetle from depositing her egg. An examination in August will detect the work of the worm in the dark and dry color of the bark, and later in the castings which have been pushed out in little heaps. During the first and second seasons the grub may easily be reached and destroyed. It is more difficult to reach him after entering the body of the tree, though a wire may follow his course and dislodge him. With proper care there is little difficulty in keeping this borer under control.

The Flat-Headed Borer (*Chrysobothris femorata*). This is a pest common to all parts of the country, attacking also the pear, plum, and other trees. Unfortunately, it does not confine its attacks to the base of the tree, but deposits its eggs within crevices or scales of the bark over the entire length of the trunk. The larva is a pale yellow grub from half to three fourths of an inch long, with a large flat head. Its habits are much like the round-headed borer, except that it is believed to mature in a single season and bore into the wood the first autumn. This is the grub which is hunted and destroyed by the woodpeckers. Sickly trees are much more likely to be attacked by this borer than those in vigorous growth. Keeping the bark clean and smooth, and painting, as in the previous case, will be a safeguard.

The Canker - Worm (*Anisopteryx vernata* and *A. pometaria*). There are two species of the canker-worm, well defined to the entomologist, and yet so similar in most respects that they have been confounded under one name. As the worms closely resemble each other in habit, size, and appearance, it is only necessary to bear in mind this difference, that the moth of the *A. pometaria* rises and deposits its eggs chiefly in the fall, while the *A. vernata* is more prolific in the spring. The fall moth, as shown at *a*, Fig. 4, and the spring moth at *b*, are both wingless females, the male moth in each case being provided with four wings. After frosts, late in the fall or early in the spring, the female moth wearily ascends the trunk of a tree and awaits the arrival

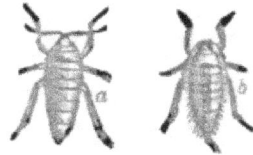

Fig. 4.

the male. The eggs are laid side by side in exposed clusters on the surface of the twigs, often a hundred, or more, in a cluster. The worm hatches nearly with the opening of the buds in the spring, and matures in from four to six weeks, when it is a dark olive-green caterpillar about one inch in length. From its method of moving it is often called the measuring worm or looper. When matured, they descend by the trunks or by silken threads, and entering the ground from two to six inches, they form a buff-colored cocoon, in which the chrysalids remain until late fall or spring. As the female moth is wingless and slow of motion, this pest is local, and is slow in distribution. But wherever it is prevalent, as in many parts of New England, if unchecked it is the utter ruin of the apple, the elm, and other vegetation upon which it feeds. Often not a vestige of foliage is left remaining upon the trees, and as this occurs in

June, during the most active stage of growth, the injury is most destructive.

The effectual remedy has been to catch the female moth at the time of her ascent. Various devices are in use, the most simple of which is the band of tarred paper, about a foot in width, tied around the trunk of the tree and kept freshly painted with tar and printer's ink, in which the moths will stick and perish. Care must be taken that the bands are tight around the trunk, also that the paint be applied in the fall, and constantly renewed, as often as it becomes glazed, whenever the ground is open, and until the worm hatches. This is a cheap and effectual method for large orchards, but it requires persistent watchfulness, and would involve too much care for a few trees. Often the moths appear in such numbers as to bridge over the band and allow their comrades to pass over their dead bodies dry shod. Increasing the width of the bands and frequent renewal of the paint would meet this difficulty. Leaden and wooden troughs, packed around the trunks of the trees and filled with kerosene oil, require much less watching and have proved effectual. These troughs are furnished by experts, and placed and warranted at the usual price of $1 per foot in diameter of the tree. To those who have but few trees this would be the safest method. Home-made troughs are liable to prove defective. Recent experiments with London-purple and Paris-green indicate that these are effectual and safe remedies. The plan is to syringe the entire tree soon after the opening of the leaves with a mixture of a heaping teaspoonful of purple to a pail full of water. For an orchard a barrel should be placed in a horse-cart and a light force-pump attached. With one man to pump and another to direct the light hose, which may be attached to a bamboo pole, all parts of a tree may easily and quickly be reached with the fine spray. It is said that this proves to be a cheap, effectual, and safe remedy. A still cheaper, less dangerous, and apparently equally as effectual remedy has recently been tried in the use of kerosene, or crude petroleum. Professor Riley, of the United States Agricultural Department, has stated a process of beating or churning two parts of kerosene with one part of soft soap, or sour milk, until they become thoroughly incorporated. After this the kerosene emulsion will dilute with water, to any desired strength. This is to be sprayed over the infested foliage in the same manner as is recommended for the arsenic preparations. The strength of the solution must be determined by trial, but it may be much

weaker in the early stage of the worm than
when it is more mature. So successful has this
application proved during the past season, that
a gentleman who has had experience in its use
has offered to clear orchards from the pest at
the rate of ten cents per tree, and thinks it can
be done at half that cost. The point is to secure
an emulsion which will afterwards mix with
water without separating. It is believed this
will prove to be one of the cheapest and most
effective insect destroyers we now have. As this
evil is still local and is comparatively slow in
spreading, owing to the disability of the female
moth, and as it is possible, by combined effort,
utterly to exterminate the insect, it is a question
whether legislative penalties should not be im-
posed upon those who neglect their trees.

Fall-Web Worm (*Hyphantria textor*). At
the South there are two generations of this worm,
but at the North the moth deposits its eggs in
broad patches on the under sides of the leaves in
early June. The larvæ soon hatch and feed in
clusters, covering their entire feeding ground
with a silken web. When full grown they are
about an inch in length, and are covered with
long straight hairs. At this stage they suddenly
scatter and feed in all directions, descending to
the ground and forming their cocoons in Septem-

ber and October. It is easy to detect and destroy them when working in clusters.

Aphides. There are many forms of plant lice, the one which infests the young growth of the apple (*Aphis mali*) hatching from eggs into tiny white lice, with the swelling of the buds. Under favoring circumstances these multiply with almost incredible rapidity; a single individual becoming the mother of many millions in one summer. But happily their destruction is comparatively easy. If prematurely hatched a subsequent frost is fatal to them. The many forms of spotted Lady Bird, or Lady Bug, destroy myriads of these aphis, and are of great service to the fruit-grower. Heavy drifting rains or showers will often clear the foliage. A decoction from the stems of tobacco, either boiled or left to soak for some days, may be used as a dip, or it may be syringed over the trees. The kerosene solution which is recommended for the canker-worm will doubtless destroy the young broods. As these lice do not eat the foliage, but puncture and suck the juices of the twigs and leaves, the arsenic preparations and other poisons are not as effectual as caustics or remedies which give off an offensive odor.

The Root Aphis (*Schizoneura lanigera*). This louse works upon the roots of the tree,

sucking the juices and causing wart-like excrescences.  Often, as the lice mature, they crawl
up the trunk and are known as the woolly aphis.
Should a tree appear sickly without cause, its
roots should be examined, and if found warty,
scalding-hot water may be applied without injury.  Professor Riley suggests also the use of
the kerosene emulsion applied to the roots.

The Oyster-Shell Bark Louse is a very common and troublesome insect, often completely
covering the trunks and branches and greatly di-
minishing the vigor of the trees.  These minute
scales, about one sixth of an inch long, cover
sometimes a hundred eggs, which hatch in May
and June; remaining for several days under
the shelter of the scales, but scattering over the
tree as the weather becomes warmer.  They are
scarcely visible, being only one hundredth of an
inch long; but being so numerous and subsist-
ing upon the sap of the tree by inserting their
sharp beaks, they cause serious injury.

Rubbing the trunks and limbs with potash
water, washing-soda, or the kerosene emulsion,
at the time the larvæ are hatching and before
they disperse, will easily destroy them.

To clear the scales at other seasons, when they
are hard and dry, will require firmer rubbing,
with a stiff brush and potash water.  Syringing
with kerosene may also prove serviceable.

The scurfy bark louse is distinct from the preceding and a smaller scale. But its habits are so similar that the same remedies may be applied.

Twig borers and pruners, leaf rooters, crumplers, and other caterpillars, are to be watched, if in any sections they become troublesome. The palmer worm is of rare occurrence, and would doubtless succumb to arsenic in the form of Paris-green.

Diseases of the apple, aside from the attacks of insects, are quite limited in number and effect. A blight, akin to that of the pear, prevails to some extent in some sections, but shows itself upon the limbs, and is pretty certain to be arrested by a quick removal of the affected part.

Parasitic fungous growth is comparatively harmless to the apple, so far as is at present known.

# CHAPTER VI.

THOUGH the pear is closely allied to the apple and may be grafted upon it (with only poor results), yet it is a very distinct and superior fruit. No one will question that the Comice and the Seckel are of more refined texture and higher flavor than any variety of the apple. It is essentially a dessert fruit, though some varieties, like the Vicar, are valuable for coddling and others make excellent preserves. It is not as healthful, or as valuable for culinary purposes, as the apple. Yet there are reasons why it will receive more general cultivation and be regarded as an indispensable fruit on every estate. There are a few good winter kinds, but it is especially a summer and autumn fruit. This early fruit is comparatively transient and is liable to suffer from transportation. Much of it perishes in the hands of the dealer. For these reasons the cost of good specimens is greatly increased. It is cheaper and less troublesome to raise our own supply.   Moreover, the trees bear when young, are of moderate size, and when vigorous **are ornamental in appearance.**   Hence every landowner requires **pear trees.**   He also requires caution, **more than he realizes, lest he plant too many trees and** too many varieties.   **It is a great** burden to have numerous kinds **which require** gathering at an exact time and varying treatment in ripening; which produce quantities in excess of private want and yet too little for profitable marketing; which are not wanted by our neighbors and are not good **for** the sick, nor even for the **cow and the pig.**   Many a suburban owner **has no other use** for them but to let them **rot.**   The remedy for this evil is simple.   Plant only such kinds **as** are of known excellence; plant very few varieties and such as ripen **in** succession, according to your definite wants.

As with the apple, we shall **be troubled** by **the** multiplicity of kinds **of** real merit, and of quality varying to suit various tastes.   The limit must be decided by each individual to suit his own family wants.   Many market gardeners **will say that** Bartlett **and** Anjou **are** enough **for** profit.   But these **do not** cover the seasons, **and** besides **they do not** give **the** differing **and the** highest flavors.   **The** following list includes the principal **kinds** of merit; quite **too** many **for**

home use, or for marketing, but from which a
selection may be made to give a constant supply
and suit every taste.

*Doyenne d'été.* — The earliest really good
kind; small, oval, fine yellow, with red cheek;
skin thin; flesh melting, juicy, sweet; prized as
the first of the season.   Last of July.

*Giffard.* — Medium   size,   pyriform;   skin
greenish-yellow, marbled  on   the   sunny side;
stalk long; flesh juicy, melting, slightly vinous,
and very good.   Middle of August.

*Rostiezer.* — Rather small, pyriform; dull
green with brownish cheek; juicy, sweet, high
flavored, and excellent.

*Clapp.* — Large, pyriform; skin smooth, yellowish-green, marbled red; flesh white, fine-
grained, very rich, juicy, vinous, and excellent.
Middle and last of August.   Tree vigorous,
open  growth, productive, hardy.   If picked
early and ripened as all, especially the summer
pears, should be, in drawers, it does not rot at
the core, and is better than the Bartlett.   It is
a fortnight earlier.   Too transient for profitable
marketing.

*Bartlett.* — Large, obtuse, pyriform; bright
clear yellow when fully ripe;  juicy, buttery,
musky perfume; very  productive, thrifty, and
unrivaled as an early market fruit.   It is not

of highest flavor, and to some tastes the musky aroma is disagreeable. Its intrinsic value is unequaled. Early September.

*Belle Lucrative.* — Medium size, roundish, pyriform; pale yellowish-green, slightly russeted; very juicy, melting, rich, and excellent. Not uniform, but when well grown it is unsurpassed. Hardy and productive. September.

*Louise Bonne.* — Large, pyriform; smooth, pale yellowish-green, with brownish red cheek in the sun; flesh melting, very juicy, sub-acid, vinous; often astringent, but excellent when well grown. Very productive and a valuable market fruit. October.

*Bosc.* — Large, long, pyriform; neck long and narrow; dull cinnamon russet; flesh white, very buttery, rich, and deliciously perfumed. October. Bears evenly and moderately; fruit is liable to drop. One of the best.

*Seckel.* — Small, ovate; dull yellowish-brown, with a russet red cheek; very fine grained, sweet, very juicy; the standard of excellence. October. Rather tardy in bearing, but becomes very productive and requires severe thinning and high culture to insure fruit of fair size. Keeps but a short time.

*Sheldon.* — Large, broad, roundish; greenish russet or cinnamon brown; flesh slightly coarse, but melting, very juicy, vinous, sweet, and excellent. October, November. When picked in season it does not rot at the core.

*Comice.* — Large, obtuse, pyriform; greenish-yellow, ripening to clear yellow; flesh white, melting, juicy, sweet, rich, and aromatic. November. One of the most promising of recent introduction.

*Anjou.* — Large, short, pyriform; greenish-yellow, with a dull red cheek to the sun; stem very short; flesh yellowish-white, buttery, melting, rich, vinous, high flavor. November to January. A vigorous, healthy, hardy, productive, uniform variety, which is regarded in all sections of the country as unsurpassed in all good qualities.

*Dana's Hovey.* — Small, or medium, obovate; pale yellow with some russet; melting, rich, juicy, high aromatic flavor, ranking with the Seckel; quality best. Early winter.

*Lawrence.* — Above medium in size; obtuse, pyriform; clear light yellow; juicy, melting, sweet, aromatic. Early winter. Productive, ripens easily, uniformly, and is one of the most reliable.

*Josephine de Malines.* — Above medium, roundish, stalk very long; color pale yellow, with some russet; flesh rose tinted, melting, sweet, juicy, with a peculiar and agreeable aroma. An excellent late winter kind.

In addition, the foregoing list may be extended with Bloodgood, Dearborn, Osband, Elizabeth, Souvenir du Congress, Brandywine, and Tyson for summer; Howell, Hardy, Buffum, Flemish, Paradise, Boussock, Superfine, Urbaniste, Mount Vernon, Clairgeau, Diel, and Duchesse d'Angoulême, for autumn and for succession in ripening; Vicar, Nelis, Aremberg, and Easter, for winter.

Dearborn is small, but of fine quality; Osband is small, productive, soon loses its quality; Elizabeth is quite small, beautiful, and excellent. Souvenir du Congress, very large, beautiful yellow, with red cheek, pyriform; buttery, melting, quality moderate; ripens with the Bartlett. Brandywine is above medium, juicy, excellent, not productive. Tyson, melting, juicy, sweet, very productive when the tree gets age. Howell and Hardy are large, excellent, and productive. Buffum is as hardy and productive as an apple; very vigorous, medium in size and quality. Flemish is very hardy at the Northern limits, where it does well, and is excellent in quality. Its liability to crack makes it worthless in many localities. Paradise is a long, pyriform russet fruit of vinous flavor; tree of straggling growth.

Boussock, a large, roundish fruit, full of juice if picked early. Superfine, medium size, very juicy, sub-acid and excellent in quality. Urbaniste, not an early but an abundant bearer; fruit of good size, pale yellow, juicy, melting, excellent. Mount Vernon, a good-sized russet-brown fruit, with a peculiar cinnamon flavor; may not prove productive. Clairgeau, one of the largest and most attractive; pyriform, yellow, shaded with orange and crimson; flesh granular, often coarse and poor. Diel, large, obtuse, slightly coarse, but melting and excellent; of late the fruit has been liable to crack and the tree is subject to blight. Duchesse d'Angoulême : this very large fruit is well known, and when well grown it ranks as very good, and is a profitable market variety. When small it is worthless. It is best on the quince stock. Vicar is a large, long pyriform fruit of moderate quality, but excellent for cooking. Its uniform productiveness and long continuance render it valuable for this purpose. Nelis : the tree is slender and straggling in growth, and liable to overbear, when it produces very small and inferior fruit. When at its best the fruit is medium in size, fine-grained, vinous, aromatic, and excellent; skin yellowish-green, much russeted. Aremberg : A most delicious winter pear, but the tree is of slow, unhealthy growth, and the fruit variable and imperfect. Easter, one of the latest and best in quality; large, yellowish, fine grained, very buttery, juicy, sweet, and rich. In order to bring it to perfection, it requires a warm soil, high culture, and careful thinning. In cool, not too dry cellars, it may be kept until April. The season is rather short for its full maturity in New England and the Northern States.

*Keiffer.* — This is a seedling of the Chinese Sand Pear, said to be crossed with some cultivated variety. Fruit large, obovate, greenish-yellow; flesh white, juicy, moderate in quality, or poor. Retaining the vigor and productiveness of the Sand, it is an improvement in quality, but is likely to be classed with the Vicar, as valuable only for cooking. It is said to be excellent for canning. It has been greatly overpraised by dealers. October to January. The vigor of foliage and remarkable early productiveness of the Sand type may encourage to hybridizing with varieties of better quality, in the hope of good results.

Besides the varieties here named there are numerous kinds which have some peculiar excellence, or local reputation. Yet no one would wish to extend the list, or to plant half the number, except for the purpose of testing, or for

exhibition. The marketman would select Bartlett and Anjou, adding Seckel and Sheldon
as his next step, and resolutely stopping with
Louise Bonne, Duchesse, and Lawrence. The
amateur requires variety and a continuous supply.
To secure this, the following eight will be the
least number, viz.: Doyenne d'été, Clapp, Bartlett, Louise Bonne, Seckel, Sheldon, Anjou,
Dana's Hovey. If his grounds will admit, he
will also want the Early Giffard, and will cast
longing eyes towards Rostiezer. Belle Lucrative
he must have, and he would like Hardy and
Howell. Bosc, Superfine, Comice, and Urbaniste are too good to pass. Vicar is wanted by
the cook, and we would like to add Lawrence
and Josephine to our winter kinds. The rejec-
tion of other varieties seems arbitrary, and thus
we see how hard it is to keep within reasonable
limits. Of course this number of trees will give
more fruit than one family can consume, however large it may be. From the list you must
then make your choice and cut down as you see
fit.

### DWARF PEARS.

The pear is dwarfed by budding it upon
quince stocks, upon which it takes readily, and
thrives when in suitable soil. This should be a
rich, retentive loam, better if inclining to clay,

when well drained. In a light, sandy, or gravelly soil the quince root is sure to disappoint. The character of the root is to be considered, it being fine and fibrous, not striking down and off like the pear, and hence requiring a constant supply of food and moisture near the surface. By giving these requisites there can be no doubt that some varieties will give the best results upon the quince root, and will continue in vigor for many years.

The prevailing impression is that dwarf pears have disappointed expectations and are not permanent. The reasons for this opinion grow out of the fact that they have been planted in unsuitable soil; that they have been thrown into premature fruitfulness and have been allowed to overbear; and chiefly that they have been starved to death. Yet it remains true that where the conditions can be secured, they are eminently suited to the amateur's wants and also are of real value to the marketman. The advantages claimed are important. The tree is dwarfed to occupy but a fifth part of the room, thus giving the amateur the privilege of a large increase of varieties. Low trees are more easily pruned and kept in form, the fruit is more easily thinned and picked, it is much less liable to be blown off; the roots of the quince are more quickly fed by surface dressing; some varieties, like the Duchesse d'Angoulême, seem to prefer the quince root, and, chief of all, the trees are thrown into early fruiting, and speedy returns are realized. Unremitting attention is requisite in order to keep a dwarf orchard in health and vigorous productiveness, but this is a condition which every fruit culturist should expect to give.

It is also important to make sure that the quince roots are planted so deep as to be entirely below the surface of the earth, not only to secure them against the attacks of the borer, but also in order to protect this more tender stock from the effects of the winter. With the earth drawn up around the collar the stock is much safer, and it is often the case that the pear will form its own roots. But in such instances the growth is unequal, the tree has lost its character, and the change is a doubtful advantage.

When the soil is right, perhaps the wisest plan would be to plant 108 standards to an acre, a distance of twenty feet apart each way. Then plant between each tree in each row a dwarf; also between each row a full row of dwarfs ten feet apart. This will give 435 trees to an acre, one quarter standards and three quarters dwarfs, with a uniform distance of ten feet between each tree. In this way the land will speedily be covered with productive trees, affording mutual protection and giving encouragement to generous cultivation. By the time the dwarfs begin to fail the standards will have become large trees, sufficient to require the entire field. If, however, there is any doubt about the fitness of the soil, or if we are inclined to shrink from constant care, it is by all means best to rely upon standards, as better able to take care of themselves. We are also to bear in mind that some varieties are in any case ill adapted to the quince stock, and only such are to be selected as are known to do well. The Angoulême, Anjou, and Louise Bonne seem to be specially suited to the quince. To these may be added Urbaniste, Brandywine, Tyson, Rostiezer, Vicar, Superfine, Hardy, Howell, Comice. The Bartlett, Seckel, Belle Lucrative, Sheldon, Bosc, and Nelis are less suited to this stock.

When the plantation is entirely of dwarfs the distance apart should seldom be less than ten feet, although by close pinching the required distance can be reduced. Standards require from fifteen to twenty feet, depending upon the system of training and the vigor of the variety. · Strong growing kinds like Bartlett will want twenty-five feet for their full natural development.

### SITUATION AND SOIL.

A slightly descending slope is most favorable, in order to facilitate drainage and the discharge of surplus surface water. But it is not essential that any particular point of the compass should be secured. Shelter from the rake of the wind is important. The pear is a companionable tree and will luxuriate when supported by other trees around it. In close garden culture a degree of humidity is preserved, and there being much less evaporation from the foliage where the strong winds are broken, the growth will be much more vigorous and healthy. There must, however, be sufficient air and sunlight to mature the wood and the fruit. If the site is high it will be an advantage to plant an evergreen belt to the windward, both for the health of the trees and also to prevent the falling of the fruit during high winds. On the other hand, a low, cold, and peaty position, subject to fogs and frosty nights, is objectionable.

A strong, retentive loam, inclining to clay, is the preferable soil. Even a stiff soil is a good basis, which can easily be lightened and warmed by the addition of stable manure. But it is essential that such retentive land be systematically underlaid with tile drains. Uniform but not excessive moisture will thereby be secured. A light soil is less promising, and will require constant enriching in order to maintain vigor. Dwarfs should not be used in such a soil, except with the free addition of heavy loam, or clay and stable manure.

Previous to planting it is very desirable that the soil should be thoroughly and deeply ploughed, so as to be in fine condition to sift in among the roots. It is a great gain also if it has been made rich by previous culture. If not, an equivalent of well-rotted manure should be worked in, but kept from immediate contact with the roots. The pear is a gross feeder and should have annual surface dressings of stable manure, wood ashes, or their equivalents. Clean culture is preferable, though some light vegetable crops may be allowed between the trees. Grains and grasses under the trees are decidedly injurious.

### PRUNING.

As a rule, the pear is symmetrical in growth and requires less pruning than other fruits. At the planting the young tree usually has six to eight shoots, the growth of the previous season, with a clean trunk of four feet, if a standard. These shoots should be shortened back to within three or four buds from the base, in order to equalize the loss of roots in transplanting, and also to insure a vigorous start and a symmetrical head. This should be done before the buds start in the spring. The central shoot must be cut just above a bud, which will preserve a straight leader and give a pyramidal form to the tree. The dotted lines in Fig. 5 show the manner of pruning in the spring after planting. No other pruning will be necessary until the following spring, when a similar process will be repeated, with a less severe reduction of the shoots, as a general rule. If any of the side branches assume a too upright habit, a bud on the lower side of the limb is selected for the terminal shoot, which will cause a more horizontal growth. On the other hand an upper bud

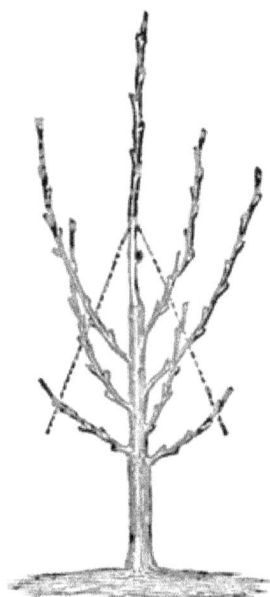

Fig. 5.

will induce an upright form. After this an annual shortening of the young shoots may be necessary, so long as the growth is vigorous. Less of this work will be required as the tree comes into bearing. Ordinary judgment will determine if the growth becomes too dense, or if the thinning out of crowding shoots and ill-shapen branches becomes desirable. Many directions have been given to guide in forming into differing shapes, as the wine-glass form, for example. But nature is usually the best indicator, and we can hardly expect to improve upon the pyramidal shape, which is the ordinary growth of the tree. For dwarfs it is obvious that the head will be formed near the ground, the pruning will be closer, and the ultimate height of the tree will not exceed ten or twelve feet.

## RIPENING THE FRUIT.

There is scarcely an exception to the rule that pears should be picked from ten days to a fortnight before they are ripe, in order to bring them to their highest quality. Some varieties, it is true, are passably good when ripened on the tree, yet none are at their best, and many which are excellent under proper treatment are comparatively worthless if allowed to hang too long. The Clapp has suffered in this respect, and has been unjustly condemned as rotting at the core. All pears should be picked as soon as signs of maturity begin to appear, or when the fruit can be readily parted without breaking the stem, generally about a fortnight before it may be said to be ripe. The Bartlett will ripen, if picked, even earlier than this, and before it has attained its full size.

It is often well to relieve an overladen tree by an early, partial picking of the most mature fruit, to the decided advantage of the last picking. The fruit should be handled with special care, and, when practicable, placed in single layers in close drawers in a cool, not too dry cellar. Exclusion of light seems to be an important point, and the highest excellence is obtained, if the fruit is brought into a warmer temperature a day or two before the texture of the flesh melts under the saccharine fermentation. The merit of many kinds depends to a great degree upon this judicious treatment in ripening. Some of the later varieties, the Lawrence for example, may be barreled and kept in a cold cellar to ripen, like winter apples. They will be improved, however, if repacked in drawers, in a warm room, a week or two before required for use.

### INSECTS INJURIOUS TO THE PEAR.

The round-headed borer, the flat-headed borer, the oyster-shell louse, the scurfy louse, the fall-web worm, and the codling moth, which have already been described as injurious to the apple, also make their attacks upon the pear. The same remedies may be used as for the apple. The plum curculio also stings the fruit of the pear to some extent. The remedy will be given under the head of the plum.

*The Pear Tree Borer (Ægeria pyri).* — This is a white grub, much smaller than the apple-borer, which feeds upon the inner bark near the base of the tree. Its presence may be detected by the fine sawdust castings, and the larvæ be destroyed by puncturing with a wire. A mound of ashes or lime around the trunk, or a coat of caustic paste in early summer, would prevent the deposit of eggs.

*The Pear Blight Beetle (Xyleborus pyri).* — Though the effect of this insect upon the small branches of the pear is similar to the fire blight, the cause is quite distinct. Upon examination the twigs will be found perforated, at the base of the buds, with pin-holes caused by a small brown beetle, about one tenth of an inch long. The remedy is to cut off the blighted limbs as soon as noticed, before the beetle has escaped, and burn them.

*The Pear Tree Psylla* is a small, yellow, jumping insect, about one tenth of an inch long, which, with its sharp beak, punctures the young growth about the middle of May, causing the sap to exude, and attracting numerous flies and ants to gather on the drooping branches. Syringe with caustic suds or with kerosene emulsion.

*The Pear Slug* is a slimy, blackish creature about half an inch long, with a small head and large, swollen anterior, — a disgusting, ill-smelling insect, which, when numerous, about the middle of June and again in August, will consume all the tissues of the leaves, stripping the trees entirely bare of foliage. Hellebore, mixed in the proportion of one ounce to two gallons of water, and syringed upon the foliage, quickly destroys the slug. Paris-green and kerosene solution would doubtless be equally effectual.

*Grasshoppers* sometimes eat the foliage of the pear and are quite troublesome. Paris-green will destroy them.

### DISEASES.

*Fire blight* is an obscure disease which has proved very destructive, especially in some sections of the West, destroying whole orchards, without the hope of remedy. In New England it has not proved so fatal, and yet in some years it is so destructive that it has caused more discouragement than all other evils combined. The prevailing opinion is that it is caused by interior fungous growth, commencing at the extremities of the tree and working downwards, with its poisonous influence, until the tree is killed. As yet, however, the most skilled microscopists have been able only to report conjectures. It is possible that parasitic growth may be only a consequence of some abnormal condition of the wood, as in the supposed condition of the peach in the "yellows," and that prevention is to be sought by imparting a healthy constitution. Certain it is, however, that the disease seems to extend from the top downwards, during the season of growth, the leaves suddenly withering and turning black on certain limbs, the bark turning dark as the disease descends. It is also certain that a quick amputation below the affected part will in most cases arrest the disease. But heroic surgery is often necessary to make sure of being below the virus. No very definite theories can be given in regard to soil, climate, or treatment, to prevent this disease. It is generally supposed, however, that too rank or immature growth, in rich, damp bottom lands favors the disease. Some varities, like Anjou, are comparatively exempt. Keiffer is claimed to be blight-proof, but the claim has been disputed. At present the quick use of the amputating knife is the only remedy.

*Cracking of the Fruit.* — Many varieties, like the old St. Michael and Flemish Beauty, are so liable to crack, that they are considered worthless in most sections. This disease is also probably caused by fungous growth, but observations are lacking to determine whether a sulphur solution applied to the affected parts would check the evil.

*Pear leaf-blight* is confined mainly to young seedlings, before they are budded by the nursery-man. Probably this is another fungous growth, which spreads over the beds in July and August, soon causing the leaves to dry up and growth to stop. No remedy has yet been discovered. Cultivated varieties do not suffer, and the main effort is to insert buds before the advent of the blight in August.

Notwithstanding the formidable list of insects and diseases, it is comparatively easy to maintain healthy trees and raise sound fruit of the pear, especially in New England.

# CHAPTER VII.

## THE PEACH.

THOUGH indigenous to a warm climate, the peach is cultivated in nearly every State of our Union. It is found, however, that a temperature of $-16°$ is pretty certain to kill the fruit buds. The same results follow a much less extreme, under some conditions, especially if the buds have been excited by a warm winter sun. A warm, protected sunny corner, or hill-side, is therefore objectionable, as likely to induce a premature excitement of the sap. Low grounds are subject to the extreme of cold. Hence it follows that high land, not to the degree of bleakness, is best. In many instances, northern slopes, which preserve a uniformly cold temperature, have been favorable, when warmer sites have failed. It has been found that a mulch of some non-conductor of heat, like shavings, applied in the latter part of winter, will retain the frost in the ground, and thus retard the sap and secure a crop.

A moderate degree of vigor of growth and a thorough ripening of the wood are essential conditions to hardiness in cold latitudes. A warm, floury loam, upon a subsoil which gives good natural drainage, is most suitable for the peach. If the soil is too rich in vegetable matter or nitrogenous manures, rank and immature wood is the result. In England, where the soil and especially the climate are usually moist, the peach is worked almost always upon the plum stock, which prefers a cooler and stronger soil. The tendency is also to dwarf the tree and to promote longevity.

In this country the results of grafting upon the plum have not been as satisfactory as would seem to be warranted in theory. Experiments in this direction have been limited, and, so far, the impression prevails that the trees are not as vigorous and healthy as those upon the natural stock. There is great difference, however, in the various plum stocks, the horse plum, the Canada, St. Julien, Damson, Myrobolan, etc., offering an important field for experiment, with the view to obtain exemption from the root disease known as the "yellows," as well as to extend the culture to moist localities.

In the great peach region centring in Maryland, it is customary to take but two or three crops from an orchard and then root up the trees.

The reasons given for this practice are that it is
more profitable to tax the trees to their utmost
while they are young and vigorous, and then
speedily to abandon them before they become enfeebled by the "yellows." By proper culture and
judicious pruning the trees may be continued for
twenty, or even for forty years, and doubtless
even this period might be doubled, as it is in
France, with proper care to nourish and keep in
health. It is, however, a tree so easily produced
and so quick to come into bearing, that it is generally best to get the vigor of youth with every
decade. The law of rotation would also indicate
that a new location would yield advantages.

Wood ashes are considered to be the best fertilizer for the peach. They furnish the principal
elements of food required, and it is believed they
impart a vigor which enables the tree to resist the
disease known as "yellows." Professor Goessman mentions two forms of fertilizer in use at the
Massachusetts Agricultural College. No. 1 consists of rectified Peruvian guano, thirty pounds;
dissolved bone-black, twenty-five pounds; sulphate of potassa (Stassfurt salt, having twenty-
five to twenty-eight per cent. of potassium oxide),
thirty pounds; crude sulphate of magnesia
(kieserite), twenty pounds. This amount for
one tenth of an acre. No. 2 contains the same

amounts of guano and bone-black, and muriate
of potash twenty pounds. Equally satisfactory
results are obtained from both applications, in
vigor and fruitfulness and apparent recovery
from the "yellows." (See Transactions of the
Massachusetts Horticultural Society, 1882, part
I., pages 120 and 130.) The simpler form of
1,000 pounds of bone meal and 300 pounds of
high grade muriate of potash, per acre, will
probably be found equally efficacious and more
readily obtained.

Trees one year from the bud are most suitable
for transplanting, and this should be done only
in the spring, in the Northern States. The wise
course is to cut the trees back to a single stem
not over three feet in height. As soon as the
buds have made a start of two or three inches,
rub off all but the one selected as likely to be
the straightest, for a new trunk. The nearer
this is to the ground the better, provided it is
above the point where it was budded. The old
stem remains for a few weeks, to which the
young shoot is tied for support, until sufficiently
strong to sustain itself. Early in July this old
trunk is cut away close down to the new shoot,
leaving no stub to prevent a speedy healing over
of the cut. No further pruning will be required
this season. The new shoot will attain an aver-

age height of about six feet, under good culture. Early in March of the season following, the lower branches are to be removed to the desired height for forming a head, giving a clear trunk of three or four feet. The top shoots are then to be shortened back nearly to the stem, leaving one top bud for a leader and four side buds for permanent side limbs. Beginning thus aright in the formation of a symmetrical head, the after process will be very simple. It is only important to remember that the tendency of the peach is to push its vitality to the extremity of the new growth, on which alone the fruit buds are formed. If left to its natural growth, it would soon become straggling, with a long, naked, and barren trunk and branches. To prevent this it is only necessary to cut back the growth of the previous season one half to two thirds of its length in March of each year. In this way the tree is kept compact and symmetrical, and a sufficient amount of new wood will remain to give all the fruit the tree can carry to perfection. Little other pruning will be found necessary, unless perchance the head becomes crowded, when a moderate summer thinning out of the weaker shoots will remedy the evil.

In the moist and foggy climate of England peaches and other fruits are largely trained upon

7

walls, in order to obtain more heat and sunlight.
For this purpose minute directions are given in
pruning, in order to maintain new growth within
the limited space and develop a sufficient number of fruit buds. This mode of training will
also afford facility for protecting the buds from
the cold of winter, by a covering of mats hung
in front. Yet it is found, in the clear, hot summer climate of this country, that the natural
form of growth is most conducive to health and
productiveness. Undoubtedly this mode of training may be practiced with success, where it is
desirable to keep the tree within limits by the side
of a walk, or where winter protection is essential.
But under ordinary circumstances the great
amount of care involved by this mode is worse
than wasted; the results are meagre, and a year
of neglect is ruinous.

Peaches may be cultivated in pots or tubs
with great success, even in our most northern
latitudes, and with certainty of an annual crop.
And this plan is to be recommended in sections
where the crop is uncertain, on account of the
moderate amount of labor involved, the pleasure
in watching the thrifty process, and the certainty of speedy and satisfactory results.

In selecting trees for this purpose choose a
medium size, one year from the bud, and cut

back to within six inches of the ground. Earthen pots at least a foot in diameter, outside measure, at the top, or better yet, a foot inside, as involving less care and larger results, and having three good sized drainage holes at the bottom, can be procured at any pottery. The holes are not to be covered with large crocks, as is usual, but rather with a small piece of inverted sod or sphagnum, which will allow the roots to penetrate to the soil beneath. The soil, which it will be well to have prepared in the fall previous, will be a mellow pasture sod, or moderately retentive loam, having but a small percentage of vegetable matter. Fresh hard wood ashes are the most suitable fertilizer to add and work in, six months previous to use, at the rate of half a bushel of ashes to a barrel of soil. Double or treble this amount of leached ashes would be required, according to its strength. Where it is difficult to obtain wood ashes a relative amount of the fertilizer, as recommended by Professor Maynard, may be used.

This compost being in fine tilth in April, and comparatively dry, it will readily work in among the roots, and pack firmly without hardening. Be careful not to plant the roots too deep, keeping them as near to the surface as they stood in the nursery. With a pestle pound the soil care-

fully, but very firmly, among the roots and around
the pot. This work cannot be too thoroughly
done, for upon this the future vigor of the tree
will largely depend. A spot is now selected,
convenient to water and having the full sun,
where the pots are to be plunged, in rows four feet
apart each way, as deeply as possible without
allowing surface water to flow into them. A
thorough saturating of the soil will now be in
order. After this, occasional waterings will be
necessary throughout the season, sufficient to
maintain a fair but not excessive degree of moisture at all times. The firm potting will make
this comparatively easy. A slight mulch outside
of the pots will also contribute to the same end.
A strong jet of water applied to the foliage will
aid to a vigorous growth and also prevent red
spider. Four or five shoots may be allowed to
grow, giving the tree a bush form, as being low,
and therefore more easily housed in winter. Just
before the ground freezes permanently, the pots
are to be raised and replunged in a cold frame,
built for the purpose. This may be simply a
pit, the sides of which are supported by a stone
wall, or by planks, with a tight roof of matched
boards. Drainage for the pit should be provided, and also ducts at each end, in order to
carry off the damp air. These may be closed in

extremely cold weather. Moderate freezing and uniform cold is desirable, but this must not extend to the degree of injuring the pots. These trees may be brought into a forcing house at any time after a short rest, and with a gradual starting may be brought to maturity of fruit by the latter part of May, and afterwards. Or they may remain in the pit until April, and then be brought out for open culture as soon as the danger from severe frosts is past. The holes at the bottom of the pots are to be cleaned, to facilitate the protrusion of new roots. Underneath where each pot is to stand two shovelfuls of cow or well-rotted horse manure are to be worked into the soil. The pots are then to be plunged as in the previous year, standing upon the manure. The young growth is to be shortened-in, usually about one half, and as an average, each shoot should develop half a dozen fruits, or from twenty-five to thirty to a tree. By careful culture these trees may be continued for several seasons, the roots being renewed at the bottom each season, and also a shift into a larger pot being made, as the size of the tree increases. A new tree would be found best after the third or fourth crop. The great danger attending this plan is in the wintering, sharp watching being necessary to guard against moisture, too severe freezing, and, on the other hand, too early a start. A cold cellar is a safer place, provided it can have some frost and be kept neither too wet nor too dry. Such culture cannot be called profitable, in the usual sense of the word, but in its influence, and in the satisfaction which it gives in yielding complete success against odds, it is fully rewarding.

In answer to the frequent question whether the peach may ever again be expected to be as certain as in former years, we have to consider that the soil is not virgin; that the climate is more arid and fluctuating, by reason of the removal of the forests, and that the "yellows" and other diseases are more prevalent than formerly. We can renew the exhausted qualities of the soil. We can surround our trees with sheltering belts. We are gradually becoming better acquainted with the nature of diseases, and are better able to apply remedies. There is therefore encouragement to plant, with a good degree of assurance of fair returns. Still, the added liability to winter-killing of the fruit buds, notwithstanding every precaution, will compel us to regard this crop as uncertain. But the conditions vary so much in the different sections of our vast country that any deficiency in one section will be likely to be fully supplied from the superabundance of some other more favored locality. The fruit is so luscious, and is so speedily and cheaply obtained, when obtained at all, that we must not relax efforts to secure it. Unlike the pear, this fruit never reaches its quality except as ripened on the tree. Hence it is the more important to raise our own supply.

The season of the peach is short. The list of varieties should consequently be short. Many varieties reproduce themselves from the seed, or are so near the parent as scarcely to deserve distinction. A few old favorites still retain their reputation, in the face of all the novelties which are continually brought forward. These may in time depreciate in merit and improved seedlings may take their place. Orchardists will confine themselves to such large, productive, and vigorous kinds as Early Crawford, Old Mixon, perhaps adding Mountain Rose and Late Crawford, but in order to obtain a continued supply and the rich variety of flavors, we must draw freely from the list. Other kinds of local merit are constantly presented, with which the amateur will gladly experiment.

The following brief list embraces the most popular kinds at the present date, which cover the entire season of ripening.

*Amsden, Alexander,* and *Waterloo* are earliest, ripening about August 1st in the vicinity of Boston; all of medium or small size, adhering considerably to the stone, but sweet and juicy. Perhaps preference may be given to the first, though Waterloo is new and may prove larger.

*Early Beatrice* follows, about August 10th; is rather small, very juicy, melting, and good; red cheek; needs thinning.

*Early Rivers.* — A large fruit, ripening the middle of August; of a creamy white color, with a delicate pink cheek, flesh melting, rich, delicious in flavor.

*Early York.* — Large, nearly white, with dark red cheek; very juicy, with rich, excellent flavor. Middle of August.

*Mountain Rose.* — Large, roundish, nearly covered with dark red; juicy and good; free stone. Tree hardy, vigorous, and productive. Middle of August.

*Cooledge's.* — Large, roundish, clear white, with red dots, deep scarlet cheek in the sun; very melting, juicy, rich, sub-acid; liable to rot. End of August.

*George the Fourth.* — Large, nearly white, dotted red, with a deep red cheek; flesh slightly red, melting, juicy, excellent.

*Yellow Rareripe.* — Large, deep yellow, juicy, vinous, one of the best. Last of August.

*Crawford's Early.* — Very large; oval with a prominent point; skin yellow, with red cheek; very juicy, sub-acid, quality excellent, but not best. Early September. Tree vigorous, productive, and the most popular variety either for the garden or orchard.

*Snow.* — Medium size; clear, creamy white skin and flesh; juicy, beautiful, and excellent for preserving. Early September.

*Old Mixon Free.* — Large; pale yellowish white, marbled red, with a deep red cheek in the sun; melting, rich, and excellent; succeeds in all sections at the North, and disputes the palm with the Early Crawford, as most valuable. Middle of September.

*Late Crawford.* — Very large; yellow with a broad red cheek; rich, juicy, vinous, and good. Deservedly the most popular late kind. Last of September.

*Foster* is a seedling from Early Crawford, which it much resembles, but has been thought to be an improvement. It is worthy of trial.

*Stump the World.* — Resembles Old Mixon and is a little later in ripening.

### INJURIOUS INSECTS AND DISEASES OF THE PEACH.

The flat-headed apple borer attacks the trunk,

and the codling moth and plum curculio affect the fruit, remedies for which will be found in their appropriate place.

*The Peach Borer (Ægeria exitiosa).* — This is a widespread and most destructive pest. The steel blue female moth, which is about an inch in length, deposits her eggs singly, on the bark of the tree at the surface of the ground. The larva soon hatches and works downward in the bark of the root, causing a copious exuding of gum mingled with worm castings. The grub is of a whitish yellow color, and over a half inch in length when mature. The winter is spent in the longitudinal grooves which have been cut in the roots, the moth issuing in the spring following. To prevent the deposit of the egg a mound of ashes or lime may be drawn up, or, still better, a band of tarred paper or similar protection may be tied around the trunk. In the fall or early spring the trees should be examined, and if the gummy exudations are found, the base should be laid bare of earth, and scalding hot water should be freely applied. This is found to be effectual, but prevention is better than cure.

A caterpillar, a leaf roller, and a few minor insects sometimes inflict injury, but not to a serious extent.

*The Peach Yellows.* — This is by far the most

serious disease to which this tree is subject. Careful microscopic observations have shown that in all cases of diseased trees different forms of fungous growth enter first on the surface of the trunk or branches, and penetrate throughout the woody tissues. The tree becomes of a sickly yellow color, the foliage is much reduced in size, the fruit ripens prematurely, and is insipid in flavor. The debatable question is, whether these fungi are the cause of disease, or only a consequence of the enfeebled condition of the tree. Working upon the last supposition, experiments have been tried at the Massachusetts Agricultural College to impart vigor to the tree, by a liberal supply of the deficient element of potash. It is stated by Professor Goessman that chronic cases of "yellows" have been recovered, after a treatment of three or four years, by the use of muriate of potash applied to the roots. It certainly appears probable that in this case, as in the analogous case of pear fire-blight, and in cases of white mildews upon the grape and gooseberry, the parasitic fungous growth is invited by some enfeebled condition of the plant. Instances of recovery, under treatment, plainly point in this direction.

If, instead of either of the formulas given above as complete fertilizers, muriate of potash

is alone applied as a remedy for the " yellows,"
Professor Goessman recommends three or four
pounds to a tree six or eight years old, spread
upon a circle of eight feet radius, but not ap-
proaching within one foot of the trunk. A thin
mulch of litter spread over the ground would insure a more uniform and a safer distribution of
the potash, which should be afterwards applied.
In this connection it should be stated that the
disease appears to be contagious, and that cases
are cited of inoculating young and vigorous
trees by contact with diseased trees. On the
other hand, repeated experiments in the free use
of potash have indicated that a vigor of constitution may be given which enables the tree to
resist the attacks of parasitic fungi. Should
this prove to be true on general trial, it would
indeed give a new phase to peach culture, and
prove an inestimable boon to the country.

## NECTARINES.

As these are only smooth-skinned varieties of
the peach, no special directions in regard to
their treatment are required. None of the varieties reach the highest standard, in quality, of
the peach, and, owing to the smooth surface of
the skin, they are greatly subject to the attacks
of the curculio. For these reasons they are not

to be recommended for open culture. The Downton, **Early Violet, Elruge, Hardwicke, Hunt's Tawny, Newington, and Red Roman** are desirable varieties, **and the** Boston is one of the most beautiful **of** fruits. **A** glass house **will** be found **to be the most** practicable mode **for** bringing this fruit to perfection. The remedy for **the** curculio **may be found** under the head **of the Plum.**

# CHAPTER VIII.

THIS tree is so hardy in all parts of the country, and the fruit is so desirable for the table and for preserving, that we might expect its general cultivation. Yet it has been so seriously affected, in recent years, by the black knot, and by the curculio, that its culture has been to a great degree neglected. But by a persistent use of remedies it is believed these evils may be met and conquered. Provided a sufficient amount of care be given, it is safe to say that many varieties will produce regular and rewarding crops. The most suitable soil is a rich, moist loam, inclining to clay. In this respect it is in marked contrast with its near relative, the peach, which prefers a warm and light soil. Hence the practice of interchanging the stocks of these two fruits, in order to adapt the roots to the peculiarities of the soil. The plum, however, does not make as large and permanent growth when budded on the peach root, as when on the plum root. A fairly retentive **loam will** do very well, with proper enriching; **but it is necessary to give generous culture, and keep down any growth of** grass, especially when **the trees are young, in** order to give vigor **to resist** disease. **In all cases of neglect,** black knot is sure to **put in an appearance.** The proper distance for planting is from fifteen to twenty feet, according to the growth of the variety, the Green Gage, *e. g.*, being small, while the Lombard and Imperial Gage are quite in contrast in **vigorous** growth.

*Green Gage.* — This is **one of the earliest to ripen, and has no superior in** quality. **It is** slow in **growth,** and in **some** seasons and **locali**ties the fruit is liable to crack. Fruit **small,** yellowish-green; flesh melting, **juicy, very sweet, and** unequaled in **flavor.**

*Lawrence's Favorite.* — **Large, yellowish**green; juicy, sprightly, vinous, melting; excellent, productive.

These two ripen about the middle of August, and are the best early kinds.

The three following are recommended as ripening about the end of August.

*Jefferson.* — **Large, oval,** yellow; **very juicy,** luscious.

*Smith's Orleans.* — **Large, oval,** reddish-purple, deep blue bloom; flesh slightly firm, juicy, **brisk, vinous; vigorous and productive.**

*Washington.* — Large, roundish-oval; yellowish-green, marked with red; sweet and rich; tree very vigorous and productive.

*Lombard* also ripens at this season, and because of its hardiness, productiveness, adaptation to light soils, and its vigor, it is much esteemed, especially for market purposes; size medium; violet red color; juicy, fair quality, but not rich; reliable.

For September, the following succeed in their order in ripening.

*McLaughlin.* — Large, roundish, russety yellow; juicy, sweet, luscious.

*Imperial Gage.* — Large, oval, green, tinged yellow; juicy, melting, rich; very productive.

*Reine Claude De Bavay.* — Roundish, oval; greenish-yellow; firm, juicy, sugary; very productive; one of the best.

*Coe's Golden.* — Large, oval, light yellow; very firm; rich, sweet, not fine-grained, but valuable for its lateness, wherever it ripens before frosts.

### INSECTS AND DISEASES OF THE PLUM.

The Plum Curculio (*Conotrachelus nenuphœ*). This is the most serious difficulty in plum culture, and the evil is widespread. The perfect insect is a dark-brown beetle, not more than a fourth of an inch long. Alighting upon a young

plum she makes a crescent-like incision under
the skin of the fruit, into which she pushes a single egg; then passing to another fruit, depositing from five to ten daily, until her stock of fifty
to a hundred is exhausted. The egg hatches in
a few days, and the larva feeds upon the fruit,
gradually boring to the stone. The grub matures in from three to five weeks, and is then
about two fifths of an inch long, and of a glossy
yellowish color. Usually the working of the
grub causes the plum to drop prematurely, and
before the larva is full grown. It is therefore
important to collect and destroy this fruit at
once. If this is neglected the larva descends
from four to six inches into the earth, and in
from three to six weeks the chrysalis is transformed to the beetle, which hibernates under the
loose bark of trees. As soon as the plum is in
blossom the moths begin
to fly, and their work commences as soon as the fruit
begins to form. Fig. 6
shows the size of the beetle, and the puncture of
the fruit. If alarmed, it
drops to the ground, feign-

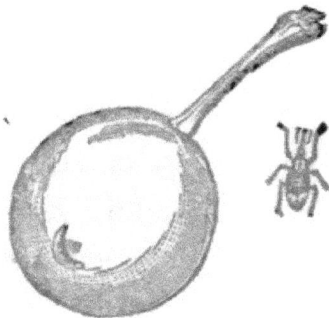

Fig. 6.

ing death. This peculiarity affords an effectual
method of destroying it. A large cotton sheet

8

(open half way up, to allow the tree to enter and stand in the centre) is spread under the tree, extending out as far as the branches. Upon a sudden jar of the tree the curculio instantly drops upon the sheet with folded limbs, as if in the repose of death. Such deceit should be quickly made a reality. Small trees may be jarred by hand. For larger trees the stump of a limb, or an iron spike driven into the tree, may serve as a place to give the blow, with a mallet, thus avoiding bruising of the bark. Bamboo poles sewed on two sides of the sheet will facilitate spreading. For large orchards this sheet might be framed and mounted on a wheel-barrow, with a padded bumper attached, so that the machine might be driven with force enough to jar the trees. It is essential to commence in season, and to follow up the process as long as there are any beetles to catch. With this care the success is certain.

The Plum-Gouger (*Coccotorus scutellaris*). This is an insect much resembling the curculio in habits, but instead of the crescent-shaped puncture, it makes a round hole in the fruit. The larva also penetrates the stone, instead of working around it. The beetle drops in the same manner as the curculio, but is more alert, and therefore is not so readily caught. It is common at the West, but has not appeared in New England.

The Plum Sphinx and several other caterpillars feed upon the leaves of the plum to some extent, but have not proved numerous enough to cause serious injury. Hand picking is, thus far, a simple remedy.

The peach borer, the flat-headed apple borer, the pear blight beetle, the apple tent caterpillar, the forest tent caterpillar, the canker-worm, the fall-web worm, and the pear slug do more or less injury to the plum, and are to be treated as suggested for the apple and pear. The codling moth sometimes injures the fruit.

The Black Knot or Plum Wart is a disease far more troublesome to the plum, and, to some extent, the cherry, than all other evils excepting the curculio. The cause of the disease is yet unknown, although it is conjectured to be fungous growth. Though the excrescences often become a harbor for insects, yet it is certain that these are not the cause. That it does not spring from an enfeebled condition of the tree would seem to be indicated by the fact that if the warts are quickly cut out and destroyed, wherever they appear, the tree retains its health. Usually this is an effectual remedy, but a thoroughly affected tree should be rooted up at once.

Leaf blight of the plum sometimes occurs in some sections, causing the premature casting of the foliage, and consequent injury. The cause and the remedy are not determined.

### APRICOTS.

The apricot is intermediate between the plum and the peach, and may be worked on either stock, but better on the former, to which it is more nearly allied. As a rule, it is earlier than the plum and the peach, and for this reason is especially desirable. But it is quite as liable to injury from the cold as the peach, and also, the fruit being smooth-skinned, the crop is usually destroyed by the curculio. Consequently it is a fruit rarely seen, and it is rightly regarded as one of the most unreliable. By a persistent destruction of the curculio this evil can be met. And by selecting a deep, high, and dry soil, not exposed to warm, winter sun, we may hope to escape the winter-killing of the buds, and thus obtain an occasional crop. The Early Golden and Red Masculine ripen early in July; the Peach, Breda, Moorpark, and Yellow Alburge, in the middle and latter part of July.

# CHAPTER IX.

## THE CHERRY.

THE early season of ripening and the refreshing acid of this fruit are points of great value. The drawbacks are that the crop is uncertain, is liable to rot, is subject to the depredation of birds, and is difficult to gather, especially when the trees are large. The intrinsic excellence of the fruit is, however, so great, the tree is so vigorous and ornamental, and requires so little care and pruning, that, if we have room, we can well afford to plant enough to give a liberal supply of fruit for ourselves and also for the birds. The cherry will thrive in nearly all good soils, preferring a rather dry, gravelly loam. Budded upon the Mazzard stock, the trees make the most vigorous growth, and attain the largest size. They should stand twenty feet apart, excepting the Dukes and Morellos, which are of smaller growth and require fifteen feet space. As an exception to all other fruits, and in order to check excessive and immature growth, a thin, green sward of grass under the tree is recommended.

The varieties of this fruit are usually divided into four classes, indicating the habit of growth and character of the fruit.

*First Class.* — Hearts.   These are vigorous and upright in growth ; fruit heart-shaped, sweet, and tender-fleshed.   Black Tartarean is one of the largest, most productive and best in this best class.   Black Eagle is similar, a little later, and not so large.   Early Purple Guigne ripens two to three weeks earlier, about the 10th of June ; is juicy, rich, and sweet, productive, and specially valuable for its earliness.   Coe's Transparent is pale amber colored, very tender, sweet, juicy, and excellent ; middle to last of June.   Downer's Late Red is juicy, sprightly, sub-acid, and continues until the middle of July, or later.

*Second Class.* — Biggareaus.   Shaped like the Hearts, but instead of the tender flesh they are firm, crisp, and breaking.   The growth is usually more spreading.   Yellow Spanish, Cleveland, Napoleon, and Rockport are good examples of this type.

*Third Class.* — Dukes.   Growth smaller, with stout, erect branches ; thick and deeper green leaves ; fruit round, usually tender. juicy, sweet, or sub-acid ; color light red to dark brown ; very hardy and productive. May Duke ripens about the middle of June. Late Duke and Louis Philippe from the middle to the last of July, and are valuable for dessert and for preserving.

*Fourth Class.* — Morellos. Like the Dukes, the trees are small, but more slender, wiry, and spreading in growth; fruit round, red, or dark red, always acid. The English Morello is the best of the type.

The cherry may be dwarfed to a considerable degree by budding upon the Mahaleb stock, and by pinching and shortening the growth, to give a compact form. In this way the Dukes and Morellos may be kept as shrubs, planted at a distance of eight feet apart, or even less. The Hearts as dwarfs would require at least ten feet distance. The advantages resulting from this low growth, in the comparative ease in protecting and in gathering the fruit, are very apparent. For garden culture, and especially if the soil inclines to be heavy and retentive, the Mahaleb stock is recommended.

### INSECTS INJURIOUS TO THE CHERRY.

A copper-colored beetle, from seven to nine tenths of an inch long, may sometimes be found during the summer months running up and down the trunks of the cherry and peach. The female deposits her eggs on the bark, and when hatched the young larva bores through the bark and lives upon the wood sap underneath. It closely resembles the flat-headed apple borer and may be destroyed in the same way.

The Cherry Bark Louse (*Lecanium cerasifex*). The scales of this insect may be found in the spring adhering to the under side of the limbs of cherry trees. These cover a mass of minute eggs. As soon as hatched the young larvæ spread over the bark of the young growth and subsist upon the juices of the twig. The scales may be removed by scrubbing with alkaline wash, and the larvæ be destroyed by tobacco water.

The Cherry Plant Louse (*Mysus cerasi*). This black louse is hatched early in the spring, from eggs deposited in the fissures and at the base of buds in the previous autumn. They come in such numbers as to cover and crowd the young foliage and stunt the growth by sucking the juices. In a few days they multiply so enormously as to make the twigs black with the mass, and to attract other insects to prey upon and destroy vast multitudes of them. Later in the season a second crop appears upon the tender leaves at the ends of the shoots. When the trees are small the twigs may be dipped in a pan of strong tobacco water or soap-suds. On large trees a drenching with kerosene solution, or tobacco, with a pump, will be effectual. The Lady Bird and its larvæ destroy great numbers of this louse, and it is a most useful ally.

The May Beetle, or May Bug, sometimes called dor-bug, is the well known dark brown or black beetle, nearly an inch in length, which comes thumping into lighted rooms in May and June. It feeds during the night upon the leaves of the cherry and plum, and when numerous does extensive injury. Its larvæ are the white grubs which burrow under grass plats, feeding upon the roots, and are often very destructive to lawns and strawberry beds. They remain in the ground for several years before reaching maturity, when the larvæ attain nearly the size of a man's little finger. Trees which have been eaten by the beetle should be shaken early in the morning, when the bugs are sluggish, and will fall and may be killed. As they are attracted by light small bonfires at night would destroy multitudes of them. They may also be entrapped by lanterns placed over tubs of soap-suds.

To some extent the tent and the fall caterpillars, the canker-worm and the pear slug, injure the foliage of the cherry.

The rose beetle, which is described in connection with the grape, often does serious injury to the foliage of the cherry. Syringing with strong tobacco water or kerosene solution is the most effectual remedy.

The plum curculio does serious injury to the cherry. As the fruit does not drop after being punctured, the larvæ mature in the ripening fruit, and a large proportion of that which is brought to market will be found to be inhabited by the worm. The sale of the fruit of course checks the increase of the insect, but it is an uncanny method, and not to be recommended. Jarring the trees, as in the case of the plum, should be persistently tried.

# CHAPTER X.

## THE QUINCE.

No variety of the quince has yet been produced sufficiently tender for use as a dessert fruit. Its aroma is also so high that it will probably never come into use except for cooking. But its excellence is so great, for this purpose alone, as a preserve, and for flavoring other sauces, that it is always in demand, and usually at a high price. It should therefore find a place in every garden. It requires a rich, deep, rather moist and retentive soil, clean culture, and yearly enriching, with stable manure spread over the surface in the autumn. Under such generous treatment the growth will be vigorous and the danger will be that the trees will be injured by the winter, in low ground. They should in such case be protected by litter or earth mounds around the roots, and by boughs stuck in the ground around the bushes, to serve as wind and sun breaks. As the quince is inclined to irregular growth and to throw numerous suckers from the trunk, a little care is required in pruning to a symmetrical form. The bushes, or low trees, may be planted ten or twelve feet apart, and under good care will continue healthy and productive for thirty or forty years. But they will speedily suffer from neglect. From one to four bushes will yield a full supply for an ordinary family.

Orange or Apple quince is the most common; is quite large, roundish, of a fine golden color, excellent in flavor, and cooks tender; ripens in mid autumn.

Rea's Mammoth resembles the previous, but is larger and perhaps less productive.

Champion. A new variety; fruit larger and more oval than the orange; quality good, bears early and said to be very productive. Promising, but not sufficiently tested as to hardiness and other qualities to warrant unqualified praise.

Portugal. Large, pyriform, very juicy and tender. The best in quality. Growth very vigorous, and on this account liable to winter-kill. It is also unproductive, which is a great drawback to its value.

Pear quince is pyriform in shape, later, and less valuable than the orange.

The Angers and Fontenay are only used as stocks.

Japan and Chinese quinces are only for ornament.

### INSECTS INJURIOUS TO THE QUINCE.

The Quince Curculio (*Conotrachelus cratægi*). This is a broad-shouldered, snout beetle, of an ash gray color, larger than the plum curculio, which appears in June, and deposits an egg in a round hole, punctured in the fruit. The larva burrows in the fruit near the surface, but does not go to the core. The beetle also feeds upon the quince, burying itself completely in the fruit. Should it be found numerous it may be destroyed by jarring the tree as described for the plum curculio.

The Round-headed Apple Borer, before described, is the borer which is so injurious to the quince. The remedies are the same, and since the quince is so much smaller and more sensitive than the apple, it is the more important that the trees should not be neglected.

The Pear Slug, a leaf crumpler, and a bag or basket worm are sometimes found upon the foliage, but are not seriously injurious.

# CHAPTER XI.

## THE GRAPE.

THIS is one of our most important and most reliable fruits, and being very hardy is specially adapted to garden culture. For the production of grapes of the highest flavor, from which the most costly wines may be obtained, it has been considered necessary to seek the light calcareous or limestone soils of high hills. Tokay wine is the product of the poor, stony, granitic land of the volcanic mountain of the same name. As the descent is to richer soils. the growth of the vine becomes more luxuriant, the fruit is larger and fairer, but the quality is more watery. The sharp slopes on either side of the river Rhine have been famous for their vine products. This soil is loose and gravelly, but has a considerable percentage of clay to give it strength. Sharp bluffs, bordering upon lakes, or flanking rivers, where a uniform humidity is obtained, and the sun pours in its warmth, are found to be favored localities. Vines trained over high rocks are

often more healthy and ripen earlier than else-
where. We may say, in general, that a high,
dry, warm, calcareous, or silicious soil is best.
But any soil which will produce a good crop of
Indian corn will also give good grapes. Full
exposure to the sun is desirable for the roots
and also for the tops. Training upon trellises on
the warm side of buildings will favor early maturity. Protection from exhausting winds, by
means of evergreen belts, or high fences, will
also prove advantageous.

In the early stages of the vine a good growth
of wood is desired. Hence the soil may be enriched with stable manure, as for corn, but not
sufficient to make excessive growth. After the
second year the object will be to supply such food
as will induce and sustain fruitfulness. As is
plainly indicated by a chemical analysis of the
wood and of the fruit, and also as has been
confirmed by practical tests, potash, bones, and
superphosphate of lime are the specific food for
the grape. Unleached wood ashes, if they can be
obtained, may be applied at the rate of four to
eight quarts to a vine, according to its size. An
annual dressing of fifty bushels of unleached
hard wood ashes per acre would probably be
sufficient for most lands. In lieu of this, three
hundred pounds of potash, dissolved and poured

upon fifty to one hundred bushels of dry muck, would give similar results. Professor Goessman, of the Massachusetts Agricultural College, recommends, as a fertilizer, supplying all the wants of the grape, for an acre, —

| | |
|---|---|
| Soluble phosphoric acid . . . . | 50 lbs. |
| Muriate of potash . . . . . | 100 " |
| Nitrate of soda . . . . . . | 25 " |
| Crude sulphate of magnesia . . | 20 " |

The phosphoric acid represents an equivalent of from 400 to 600 pounds of the superphosphates of commerce. Continued experiments by Professor S. T. Maynard incline him to increase the nitrate of soda to 75 or 100 pounds, according as wood growth is desired. He would also increase the muriate of potash (high grade) to 150 pounds.

As a simpler and economical form and at the same time a complete fertilizer for most kinds of fruit, he recommends fine ground bone and muriate of potash in the proportions given in the chapter upon manures. To this a surface dressing of 300 pounds of guano might be added, in case the wood growth proved insufficient. Bone meal is deservedly held in high esteem, and this, added to the muriate, is probably the simplest and best specific that can be given. Where vines are planted at an average distance of eight feet apart, this quantity would give about two pounds of the mixture to each vine. Cultivators aiming for heavy crops and fruit of superior quality will doubtless increase this amount, with advantage. Bone-black from the refineries may be used as a substitute for bone meal, provided it can be found at a moderate price. It is usually bought up by dealers, who know its value as an absorbent. A clean and floury condition of the soil should be preserved in order that the roots may have summer warmth and air.

Vines not over two years old are best for planting. Early fall is undoubtedly the best time to plant, provided a little coarse manure is thrown over the surface to keep out the frost. A more vigorous growth will thus be secured in the following season. After November 1st it would be better to delay planting until April. This work should be done when the soil is dry, spreading the roots evenly in all directions, stretching them out their full length, and at the depth of four to six inches below the surface. The earth is to be pressed very firmly about every root, leaving the vine established as nearly as possible as if it had not been moved. In the spring the vine is invariably to be cut back to three eyes, however long the top may previously have been. As the eyes start, the two weakest

are rubbed off, leaving but one strong shoot to
make the future cane. This shoot is tied to a
stake and allowed to run up perpendicularly,
making a growth of six to eight feet the first
year. In the spring following, this cane is again
cut back to three eyes in order to give a strong
cane, with abundant root force. But at this
point the treatment will depend upon the training to be adopted.

No other fruit requires so much pruning as the
grape. The tendency of the vine is to make
wood, to climb to the tops of trees, or whatever
else it may find for support, showing its greatest
vigor at its extremities, at the top. Vines thus
allowed to run, as upon arbors and buildings,
are vigorous, and as they attain age are often
fruitful. But the fruit is shaded and choked
with too much wood, and is always inferior in
quality. To remedy this tendency to growth and
throw the strength into the fruit, various methods
of training, of pruning, and of fertilizing have
been adopted. It is well understood that sap
flows with most force in a perpendicular upward
course. Hence the leading shoot will easily
keep the lead and never cease to make growth.
In countries where the rain-fall is small and the
soil is loose and thin, all that is required to
check growth and produce fruitfulness is to bend

the canes in a hoop form, and support with a short stake. The branches are allowed to swing free, and to arch over by their own weight and the weight of fruit. Where there is more vigor, more systematic artificial training is necessary. The method commonly recommended is the perpendicular trellis system. This consists in a supporting trellis of four No. 14 annealed, gal-

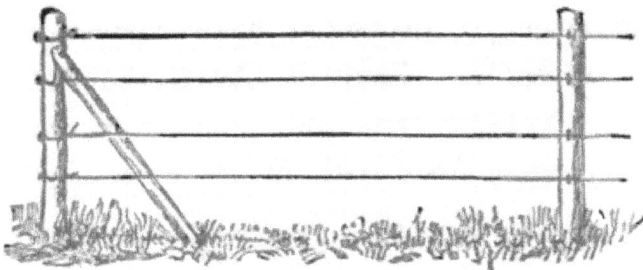

Fig. 7.

vanized iron wires stretched upon posts as in Fig. 7. The lower wire, which is the support for the arm of the vine, should be at least a foot and a half above the ground. The second wire, which supports the fruit, should be from eight to ten inches above this, and the two upper wires may be a foot apart. This trellis is not constructed until the third season after planting, when the first crop is taken. During the second year the training is precisely like the first, excepting, in case two arms are to be trained, that two shoots are allowed to grow perpendicularly instead of one. Any inequality of growth may be counteracted by pinching laterals which are too vigorous. The object is to obtain a well-ripened arm at the end of the second season, or two arms, if so preferred. These are to be cut back in November to about six feet in length, and with plump fruit-buds evenly distributed about a foot apart on the cane. During the winter the vines will lie upon the ground, and if protected by evergreen boughs they are safer. Early in April the canes are tied to the lower wire, and each bud is expected to produce a shoot, with one or more clusters of fruit.

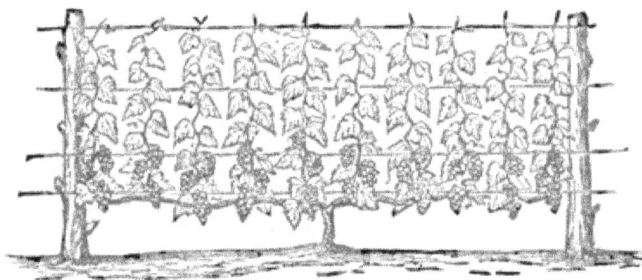

Fig. 8.

Fig. 8 shows the appearance of a vine with two arms at the end of the third season. All the new growth is carefully tied to the upper wires as the leaders and laterals are closely pinched and the space is filled. In November this new growth is to be pruned back, leaving bare arms as in the previous year. The only difference is in the selection of the fruiting-bud for the following year.

Fig. 9 represents the spur as pruned at the end of the third year. The two base eyes, *b* and *c*, may be

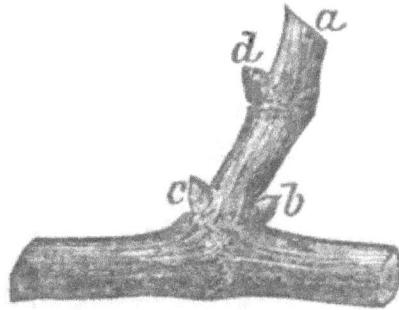

Fig. 9.

too small to be trusted for fruit, and are to be removed when they start. The eye *d* will make the fruiting shoot of the fourth year, and will be pruned back again in November, as in Fig. 10. The eye *b* is to bear the fruit the following year and the small eyes, *a, a,* are to be rubbed out. Thus the spur increases about one

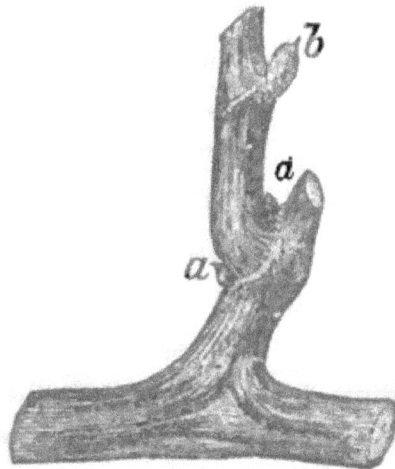

Fig. 10.

inch annually. This is objectionable, but it can often be obviated by finding a base eye sufficiently strong to make a fruiting shoot, or by a gradual renewal from a base eye, if the spurs become too long. It is undoubtedly true that as canes advance in age they become stiff and break unevenly. And, in addition, the fruit clusters gradually diminish in size. Many good cultivators have felt that large clusters were of so much importance to their sales that they have adopted the annual renewal system, as it is called. This consists in selecting a vigorous shoot near the base of the vine, and training it up perpendicularly until it reaches the required length of the vine, when it is stopped. In the mean time, the old cane is bearing its fruit. After stopping the new shoot it will throw out laterals, which are in turn to be stopped when about a foot long. Plump lateral eyes will thus be developed, and it is from the one nearest the base of each that the largest fruit is expected. Splendid results have followed this method, and first prizes are usually obtained in some such way. But manifestly a large amount of wood growth is involved in the plan, and it is questionable whether the young shoot does not draw too much vigor from the bearing cane, especially if the practice is persisted in year after year. Beyond doubt an increased quantity of nitrogenous matter would be desirable, if such annual growth is required. Experiments are wanting to show how long such a system can be practiced with success. An occasional renewal is the better way for home use, giving sufficiently large clusters and of better quality, because less succulent and ripening better. When it is desirable to cover high trellises or buildings, a modified form called the Thomery, from the French village where it was in use a century ago, may be adopted.

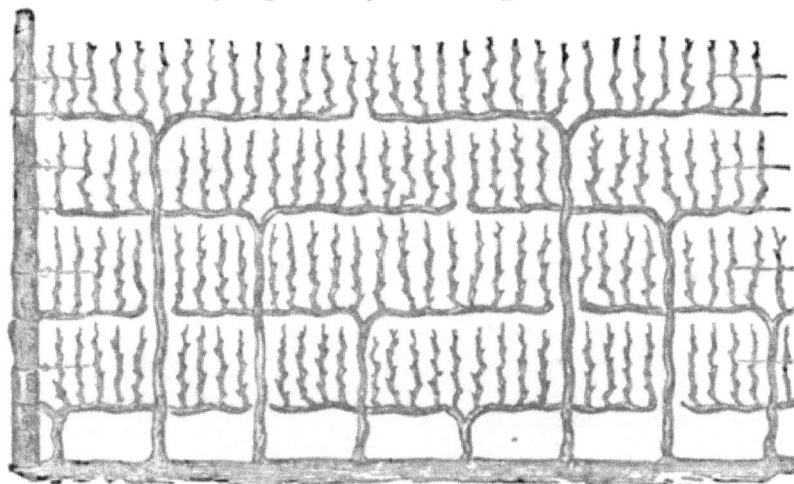

Fig. 11.

Fig. 11 illustrates the method with two arms. It will be seen that while the upright flow of sap is checked by the horizontal position of the arms, yet the young shoots retain the upright position, and those nearest the centre trunk do practically receive a perpendicular flow. However simple and beautiful this system may appear in theory, in practice it does not fully overcome the evil it was designed to meet, and it involves more labor and attention in tying and pruning than is likely to be given, in general culture. Instead of the upright trellis, a more simple mode of training is to tie the cane horizontally to a wire stretched three feet from the ground. Two other wires stretched on either side and eight inches distant from the cane, which are supported by cross-pieces at each post, will be for the support of the fruiting branches. Most of these will fall over naturally, or may easily be bent into position, with an occasional tying. The weight of the fruit will soon hold the branches to the side wires for support. In this natural and drooping position it will be seen in Fig. 12 that

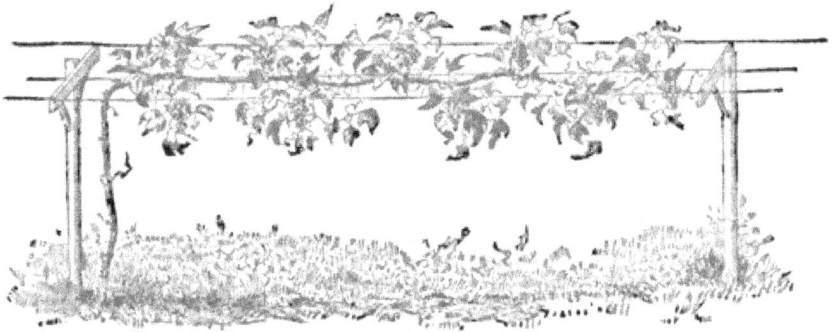

Fig 12.

the flow of the sap will be equally distributed and to the greatest advantage of the fruit. When the branches have made four or five leaves beyond the fruit branches, the shoots are nipped, to stop the growth of wood. Laterals will soon start, which are in turn to be nipped at one leaf or more, according to the density of foliage.

No more wood growth is to be permitted, the strength of the vine being now concentrated in developing the fruit. This mode of training is well adapted to vineyard culture, the rows being eight to ten feet apart in order to obtain a free play of air and sunlight. A more common method among vineyardists is to twist or bend the cane to posts and compel the branches to support themselves as they may, in a more or less pendent position. The usual distance for these posts is about eight feet each way, for strong growing kinds. Six feet would be sufficient for the Delaware.

The advantages of the post system are that the air and sunlight have free play on all sides, and the wood becomes thoroughly mature; the twisting and bending of the cane checks the upward flow of sap, and the fruiting shoots assume a pendent position, which also tends to develop the fruit. Two posts, three feet apart, with cross-pieces, to give firmness, and also convenient places for tying, are also recommended. The object is a firm support, and a form which shall check too strong an upward flow of sap. Any system which shall secure these two ends with least labor is best. It is all important, whatever system is adopted, to secure a thorough ripening and hardening of the wood. When this is obtained there is little danger that the vines will be injured by the winter.

In covering arbors and buildings, the practice has been to allow altogether too much growth of wood, and to neglect almost entirely to check the young shoots. If good fruit is desired, it will be necessary to establish permanent canes about four feet apart, on the sides and top of the arbor, or upon frames six inches in front of buildings, which canes are to be evenly supplied with eyes, or spurs, about a foot apart. Fruiting branches will start from these spurs, as described for the horizontal arm, which are to be nipped in midsummer and pruned in November in the same manner. By such systematic training and pruning alone can we hope to secure good fruit in addition to the shade.

### GRAPE HOUSES.

No other fruit is raised so easily, or retains its quality so well under glass, as the grape. With simply a roof of glass, the back being always open in summer, not only our best native varieties can be matured with certainty, but also the European kinds can be safely brought to perfection. The slight increase of heat and also the protection from excess of rain and from the cold dews of night are advantages sufficient to insure complete **success**. Very little modification of the out-door culture is required. The vines **are** planted more closely together, **in** order to economize space to the utmost, **the single** canes running up about a **foot below the glass** roof, and **four** feet distant from **each other.** The mode of training is precisely **like** the three horizontal wire trellis system, as seen in Fig. 12, page 136. The trellis will of course follow the angle of the roof. The same directions in regard to checking **and** pruning **are** to be followed as have been given for open culture.

By making the house more permanent, open-ing and closing in order to have complete con-trol of the air, still greater advantages **are ob-**tained. Early closing of the ventilators **and** free showering a **few** hours before **sunset and** early in the morning will **cause** luxuriant growth in the early part of the season. **In a** close house it is easy to secure complete exemption from all diseases. As the season advances water is with-held, and a free circulation of air is given **in** dry weather. The **latest** and most **delicate** kinds, like the Muscats, can be **cultivated with** perfect success in a cold grapery, and **with a** certainty which **does not pertain to any** out-of-door fruit. With **the aid of heat, and by suc-**cession and retarding houses, **it is practicable to** have grapes throughout the entire year. With this artificial protection of glass, and with a dry air during the period of inflorescence, most of the European varieties will set fruit too thickly, and not only clusters must be removed, but also one half, or even more of the berries must be cut out from the remaining bunches, soon after setting, and before they begin to crowd. This is the only tedious item in the whole process. It is wise to prepare a border about two feet in depth, and well supplied with potash, bones, and horse manure, for vines running into houses. By furnishing this excess of food, and by close pruning, enormous crops can be concentrated within a limited space.

*The ringing process* is a curious mode of developing and hastening the maturity of the fruit. It consists in the entire removal of the bark just below a fruit cluster, about a month before its time of ripening. Fig. 13 shows the position of the cut, which may be half an inch in width. The sap, ascending

Fig. 13.

through the pores of the wood, sustains growth. But the descending, elaborated sap, which passes down between the wood and bark, is arrested by the cut, and concentrated in the shoot and fruit. Fig. 14 shows the enlargement above the cut, caused by this arrest. Fruit is invariably found to be not only increased in size, but also hastened a week or two in maturity. To a limited extent, and on scattering branches, this experiment may be tried. But it is evident that the eyes below the cut will suffer for the following year, and the vine itself would be injured if the practice were general.

In addition to the directions previously given, which guard against fruiting during the second season, a word of caution is necessary, lest the vines are overtaxed with fruit when they are young. Thin out the bunches as soon as they are set, and aim for a moderate crop of superior quality.

Fig. 14.

### VARIETIES.

In 1820, Mr. John Adlum introduced the Catawba, and the Isabella followed soon after. These were the only well-known kinds at the

North, until the Diana was added in the year
1843. The Concord followed ten years after;
and since this the number of seedlings has been
legion. It will be useless to even name a multi-
tude of varieties which are crowded upon the
market. A short list of those which are well
tried and reliable is here given, and also a few
notes respecting some of the novelties.

*Brighton.* — A new variety with large, rather
loose bunches; large, rose-colored berries of excellent quality, ripening about with, or after the
Concord. Rather late, and somewhat subject to
mildew, but worthy of a place.

*Concord.* — On account of its vigor, hardiness, productiveness, and fine appearance, it has
been cultivated at the North more than all
others combined. It is not best in quality, but
has been ranked as most valuable. Seedlings
from the Concord are earlier, and may yet
supersede it.

*Delaware.* — This little grape heads the list
for family use. It is small in cluster and berry,
not strong in growth, and somewhat liable to
mildew. Yet with good culture, generous feeding beyond the requirements of coarser kinds,
and a careful use of sulphur, it is pretty sure to
give a good annual supply of delicious fruit.
Presumably it is a seedling from the European

red Traminer. Though succeeding in field culture in some sections, it does not weigh sufficiently to sell with the Concord. Ripens early
in September. The vine improves with age.

*Lady.* — A hardy iron-clad, which resists mildew; ripens very early, bunches small; berries
medium, greenish-white, sweet, and of fair quality. Desirable for its earliness.

*Moore's Early.* — A seedling from the Concord, and from ten days to a fortnight earlier,
larger berries, and in other respects similar. It
appears to be very productive, and most promising. On account of its earliness it may take
precedence of the Concord.

*Worden* is another Concord seedling, ripening
ten days earlier, and is of better quality than its
parent, and therefore held in high esteem.

To this list may be added Catawba and Iona,
two dark red varieties of highest flavor, but too
late except for favored localities; Isabella, an
excellent black, but also late and uncertain;
Hartford and Champion, two very early and
productive black grapes of inferior quality;
Creveling, black, ripening with the Concord,
of an agreeable plum-like flavor, but unproductive, bunches loose; Diana, compact bunches,
berries pale grayish red, very high flavor, juicy,
sweet, little pulp; keeps long. Its value is

greatly lessened by ripening unequally in the same bunch, and varying in different localities.

*Rogers Hybrids.* — These numerous seedlings vary entirely in characteristics, but it is doubtful if any of them will be permanently valuable in northern latitudes. Lindley and Salem, of a rose color, and Wilder, a large black grape, are among the best of these.

The following new kinds are for trial: —

*Jefferson.* — A dark red berry, with little pulp, and of highest flavor. Appears to be vigorous, healthy, but rather late.

*Vergennes.* — Bunch and berry large, light red, very good quality, ripens early; vine vigorous, healthy, and productive; quite promising.

*Early Victor.* — A Kansas grape, said to be very hardy, early, and prolific; bunch small; berries black with a blue bloom; sprightly; rather acid fruit.

*Duchess.* — Bunch large shouldered; berries medium, greenish-yellow, juicy; sprightly, late, and subject to mildew.

*Pocklington.* — Large, golden yellow bunches have been exhibited, but it appears to be late and unreliable.

*Prentiss.* — A prolific, greenish-white grape of excellent quality, and esteemed in some localities, but liable to mildew.

*Niagara.* — This new white Lockport grape is reported to be remarkable for its vigor, hardiness, and productive qualities. The bunches are of good size, rather long, compact, and attractive; quality good, becoming very good at the time the Concord is ripe. Great confidence in the intrinsic value of this variety has been shown by careful observers, and the results of its speedy trial will be watched with interest.

*Francis B. Hayes.* — Still another white grape of excellent quality, and in the hands of Colonel Moore, its introducer, it appears to be healthy and productive, ripening a little later than his Moore's Early.

For culture under glass, Black Hamburgh is the leading kind, to which may be added, for black, St. Peter's, Black Prince, Black Muscat; and for late keeping, Lady Downe's and Trentham Black. For light color, White Frontignan and Grizzly Frontignan are hardy, uniformly productive, and have a high musky flavor. Buckland's Sweet Water, Syrian, and White Nice are also adapted to a cold house. Bowood Muscat and Muscat of Alexandria have a rich Muscat flavor, are very large and superb, but require a higher temperature and a separate house for perfect development.

### INSECTS INJURIOUS TO THE GRAPE.

The Grape Phylloxera (*P. vastatrix*). This is a native American louse, which has been exported to Europe, and has become immensely destructive to the foreign varieties of grapes, which are much more liable to its attacks than our American kinds. The louse develops in two forms, one of which infests the leaves, puncturing and producing galls on the under side, which they inhabit, rapidly multiplying and extending their operations. The other and more hurtful form subsist upon the young rootlets, causing little swellings which gradually extend, to the utter ruin of whole vineyards in France and other countries. Recently it has appeared upon the European varieties cultivated in California, and it is feared will prove very destructive. It is also to a considerable degree injurious to our native kinds, and to some varieties more than to others. The Concord and Clinton types are comparatively free. The gall-producing type may easily be controlled by gathering the infested leaves. In planting young vines, the roots should be carefully examined to see if knotty swellings are upon the roots; if so, the lice may readily be destroyed by dipping in hot soap-suds or tobacco water. It is difficult to reach the lice upon established vines, although various modes are suggested. Professor C. V. Riley thinks the kerosene solution poured freely upon the roots will prove efficacious. Carbolic acid, in the proportion of one part to fifty or one hundred parts of water, poured into holes around the vine has proved advantageous. Bisulphide of carbon, if introduced into the soil, two to three ounces to a hole, and several holes to each vine, is said to permeate the soil and kill the lice, without injury to the vine. It is very volatile, inflammable, and explosive, and should be carefully handled. Potash fertilizers and also salt are found to be useful. Sandy soils are said to be less liable to have the insect. As our native vines are comparatively exempt, they are recommended as stocks upon which to graft the European varieties and the Delaware types, should they become liable to attack.

The Green Grape Sphinx. This is a large, pale green caterpillar, about two inches long when the larva is full grown, which is very voracious; a few of them being sufficient to strip a vine of foliage. It is easy to see their work and to destroy them. Other varieties of Sphinx and large caterpillars are also found to some extent, which are to be hand-picked and destroyed.

The Beautiful Wood Nymph (*Eudryas*

*grata*). The larva of this beautiful moth is often quite destructive to grape foliage. When mature the worm is about an inch and a half long, pale bluish black, crossed by orange bands, and with orange head dotted black. It feeds upon the woodbine as well as the grape. The Pearl Wood Nymph and the Eight-Spotted Forester produce larvæ much resembling the Beautiful Wood Nymph.

The American Procris. This is a much smaller caterpillar, about six tenths of an inch long at maturity, in August; slightly hairy, and of a yellow color. The larvæ feed in line on the under side of the leaves, upon the soft tissue, when young, but devour all except the large veins, as they grow. They are more destructive at the West than in New England. The last four, and also several other forms of caterpillar, if numerous, may be destroyed by syringing with Paris-green, one teaspoonful to two gallons of water, or with hellebore, one ounce to two gallons.

The Grape-Vine Flea Beetle is a destructive beetle, varying in color from steel blue to blue, about three twentieths of an inch in length, which commences its work by eating into the substance of the buds as soon as they swell. It deposits its eggs on the under side of the young leaves, and in a few days the larvæ hatch and feed upon the leaves for three or four weeks, attaining to a little more than three tenths of an inch in length. In the fall the beetle finds shelter under leaves, pieces of bark, or in the earth immediately around the vine. Removing the rubbish and strewing air-slacked lime or unleached ashes would destroy them. In the spring jarring the vines, in early morning, will bring them to the ground, when they may be killed. Syringing the foliage with Paris-green and other solutions will destroy the larvæ.

The Rose Beetle or Rose Bug (*Macrodactylus subspinosa*). This is a dull yellowish beetle, about one third of an inch long, with long sprawling legs, which often appears in swarms at the time the grape and the rose are in blossom. They do great damage to the cherry and the rose, and are specially attracted by the fragrance of the grape blossoms, which they quickly destroy. They remain until about the middle of July, when the female deposits about thirty eggs in the earth, and the larvæ feed upon such roots as are within reach. Hand-picking is a tedious process when the bugs are numerous, but it has been practiced as the only effectual remedy. In the morning the bugs are sluggish, and may be jarred into sheets and thrown into a dish of kerosene. Covering the vines with mosquito netting has been resorted to in many places. Whale-oil suds have no appreciable effect upon the bug. Kerosene will kill it, but whether it can be used with sufficient strength to be effectual, without injury to the vine, is yet to be proved. Paris-green should also be tried.

The Leaf-Hopper or Thrip is often a troublesome little insect about one eighth of an inch long, wingless in its early stage, but acquiring wings as it matures and becomes able to fly from vine to vine. It feeds upon the under side of the leaves, especially those of delicate foliage like the Delaware, and often increases to such numbers as to do serious injury. In glass houses it is easy to destroy them by fumigating with tobacco when they are young. As they mature they are much tougher. Syringing with tobacco water, hellebore, and other decoctions, in early summer, is serviceable. Carrying lighted torches through the vineyard and at the same time rustling the foliage will attract and burn the mature winged hopper. It is much easier to destroy them when they are young and delicate.

Root borers are troublesome in some sections, especially the Grape Root Borer (*Ægeria polistiformis*), in North Carolina and in the Middle and Western States. A mound of earth or a band of tarred paper would prevent the deposit of eggs.

The Grape-Berry moth is imported from Europe, where it has long been destructive to the fruit. Early in July the young larva enters a berry and feeds upon the pulp, entering two, three, or more berries, if not satisfied with one. When full grown and about one fourth of an inch long, it forms its cocoons upon the leaves of the vine, cutting out a flap which it turns back on the leaf and then lines the inclosure with silk. These cocoons, and also all infested fruit, should be gathered and destroyed.

Red spider seldom does serious injury to the grape in open culture, unless the season is exceptionally hot and dry, when the more delicate varieties suffer. Syringing the under surface of the leaves with sulphur or kerosene solution and whale-oil soap-suds will destroy these minute insects.

### MILDEW.

There are several forms of fungous growth which affect the foliage and the fruit of the grape, in some seasons and upon some varieties, with most destructive results. It is an unsettled question whether the attack of this parasitic growth depends upon an enfeebled condition of the vine, and some disruption of the tissues, a certain preparation of the surface for the seed, so to speak, or is, on the other hand, the independent cause of all the evil. Certain it is that the more delicate varieties are much the most subject to the disease, and these especially so in some soils, and when in weak condition. It is noticeable with what rapidity many kinds of mildew spread upon decaying vegetation. It is also certain that a warm, humid state of the atmosphere greatly facilitates the rapid growth of fungi. Sections subject to heavy dews at night are much troubled with mildew. A projecting coping which covers the vine from night dews is said to protect from fungus. We may avoid the evil by selecting varieties which have tough foliage and are least subject to attack. But we shall thus exclude our best kinds. We can give special care to furnish specific food, like phosphates and potash, and thus give vigor to resist. Thorough drainage and protection from rains and dews are preventives. Last of all we can kill the fungus. It is a low form of vegetable growth, and consequently sensitive to any influence that is destructive to vegetable life. Any drying powder, simple wheat flour for example, will, in some conditions, seem to absorb the moisture, or smother the delicate mildew growth and hold it in check. This, however, is not mentioned as a remedy, but only as indicating the sensitiveness of the microscopic plant. Small as it is, we must resort to more powerful measures to hold it in check. The fumes of burning sulphur are destructive to *all* forms of vegetable life. But the slow oxidizing of sulphur will give off a gas which proves fatal to such delicate growth as mildew, without perceptible injury to the foliage of the vine. Hence the well-known remedy of dusting the foliage with flowers of sulphur upon the first appearance of mildew. Should the weather continue damp and warm it may be difficult to prevent the spread of the disease, but there is no doubt it can be greatly held in check. A kind of bellows is made which will facilitate the even distribution of the sulphur among the leaves. This remedy is called in question by high authority, and it must be admitted that in wet weather, when mildew is most prevalent, a very inadequate amount of sulphurous gas is supplied in the open vineyard from such dusting. A more effectual and speedy remedy will be found in a solution made as follows: To a peck of quicklime add five pounds of sulphur, and slack with hot water in a barrel, keeping a full supply of water, to prevent burning. Afterwards fill the barrel with water, and let it settle. This liquid may be lightly syringed through the foliage at full strength, without injury, but it is better to reduce with an equal amount of water, and use a larger quantity. When the liquid is nearly exhausted the barrel may be refilled with warm water, the lime being thoroughly stirred, and thus a second, but weaker run, may be obtained. This is the most speedy and effectual remedy in aggravated cases. In a close house, brimstone or sulphur may be melted in a skillet, with a kerosene lamp, provided extreme care is exercised to prevent flame, and the giving off of sulphuric acid gas, which is so fatal. Indeed, it will be best not to allow the fumes to pervade the house very freely at the first, but to make a gradual trial of its strength. It is a powerful remedy to which low forms of insect life, like the red spider, will also yield. But it should be heated with great caution. Dry rot is another form of fungus which attacks the berries, causing premature discoloration, and final shriveling. It is most prevalent in damp and heavy soils, and it has been suggested that the remedy should be sought in the soil, and in giving elements of nourishment. Downing recommends sulphate of lime (plaster of Paris) as a specific, and some cases of perceptible effect are reported. As the fungous growth is internal, outward applications are apparently useless.

# CHAPTER XII.

## THE CURRANT.

In ease of culture, certainty, and productiveness, this fruit excels all others. It is also one of the most healthful acids during the heat of summer. Its compact form of growth adapts it to garden culture, between rows and under the partial shade of trees. Clean culture and a rich soil will give by far the best results. The fruit is produced upon shoots two or more years old, and it is important that a succession of vigorous branches should be maintained. Owing to the dryness of our climate it is not desirable to prune to a tree form, with a single clean stem for a foot or more above the ground, as is frequent in England. It is better to prune to bush form, allowing new shoots to start from near the ground to take the place of old branches as they become stunted. In this way of renewal, and by a fall surface dressing of stable manure, the bushes may be kept in health for a score or two of years. The proper distance for planting is four feet each way. Three feet has been a common distance, but under generous culture the bushes become crowded. The white varieties are less acid, and therefore are preferred by some for the table. White Grape is the best of this class. Dana's White is larger, but more acid, a more showy market variety. The red class has several varieties of merit.

Cherry is of largest size, cluster rather short, quite acid; moderately productive, profitable for market.

Versailles closely resembles the Cherry, but is supposed to have longer bunches, and to be less acid. The difference, if any, is so slight that competent judges refuse to recognize it.

Fay's Prolific also resembles the Cherry, but appears to be more productive, and to set longer clusters. Promises well and deserves trial.

Victoria. Fruit larger than Red Dutch, clusters very long, rather late, and hang a long time. Quality good, not acid; valuable for its lateness, and other merits.

Red Dutch. Long clusters, medium size, quality good; productive.

Black Naples is the best of the blacks, and is prized by many for jams and jellies.

INSECTS ATTACKING THE CURRANT.

The Currant Worm. There are two species of this worm, the one imported from Europe (*Nematus ventricosus*) being larger and much more destructive than the native, saw-fly larva. When first hatched the European larva is of a whitish color, and about one twelfth of an inch long. It changes in color to plain green, and increases to three quarters of an inch in length, while the native is but half an inch long and always green. Two broods of larvæ are hatched in a season, and as they multiply in great numbers and are enormously voracious, they would ruin a plantation in a single season, unless checked. Fortunately, they are easily destroyed by sprinkling the bushes with hellebore mixed in water, in the proportion of one ounce to a pailful. Strong soap-suds and the kerosene solution are also effectual. Air-slacked lime dusted upon the bushes is a check. Strong tobacco water is an excellent remedy.

The Currant Span Worm is a larger caterpillar, about an inch long, whitish, with yellow stripes and numerous black dots, and readily distinguished by its arching loop at every step. It is not so easily destroyed as the worm previously named, and hence the decoctions should be of double strength.   Fortunately, it is by no means so numerous.

Currant Borers.   Two species of borers, a native and an imported, burrow up and down the stem, feeding upon the pith, indicating their presence by the sickly look of the leaves.   The moth escapes from the stem early in June.   All hollow stems should be cut out and burned, in the fall or early spring.   Vigorous plants are seldom injured.

When a plantation becomes infested with bark-lice and scales, it is possible to cleanse with strong alkaline washes, but it is usually better to root out and burn the old plants, and begin anew with fresh and healthy bushes.

### THE GOOSEBERRY.

In the moist climate of England, the goose-berry is cultivated with great success, and it is highly prized as a dessert fruit.   All these Euro-pean varieties are subject to parasitic growth, commonly known as mildew, when cultivated in this country.   In the main we are limited to a few native varieties, which are comparatively exempt from this disease.   These are much below the English varieties in quality, and are used mainly for pies, sauces, and jams.   Some cultivators have good success with the English kinds by planting under the shelter of fences, buildings, or trees, and by mulching with salt hay, or salted marsh-hay, for the purpose of securing uniform dampness. The good results obtained seem to indicate that mildew upon the gooseberry depends upon the enfeebled condition of the plant in a dry climate.

Crown Bob, Roaring Lion, Whitesmith, and Green Ocean are standard English varieties. Windham's Industry is a new kind, of unusual vigor, which may prove to be adapted to our climate and therefore desirable. Of native kinds Smith's Improved and Downing are the largest and best. Mountain and Houghton's Seedling are smaller, very productive, and free from mildew. The gooseberry is subject to the attacks of the currant worm and the span worm, for which the same remedies should be applied. A larva also burrows into the fruit, attaining a full size of nearly three quarters of an inch. A very small midge also deposits its minute eggs upon the fruit, and the tiny larvæ burrow within. The presence of these insects is shown by the withering or the premature ripening of the fruit, which should be picked before the moth escapes.

# CHAPTER XIII.

EMINENTLY this is a home fruit. The best varieties are so soft as to suffer by transportation and by keeping. The plants are specially adapted to garden culture, and when properly treated are certain, productive, and permanent. It requires less care than the strawberry, is more easily picked, and by most persons is preferred, for its high flavor. It deserves a place in every garden, and also more extensive and careful culture for local markets. In most of our large cities the supply of a good quality of this fruit has been less than the demand, and hence the price has been very remunerative. A rich and deep, rather moist loam, not inclining either to gravel or clay, but what would be called a mellow, retentive garden soil, is best. The planting of the red varieties should be in rows four feet apart, and three feet apart in the rows. It is better to cut the plants down within six inches of the ground, in planting; thus obtaining three to five strong shoots from the root, for next season's fruiting. No care is necessary, except clean culture and the removal of any extra shoots with the hoe.

All of this class which are worthy of culture are too tender to be subjected to winter exposure. It is a simple, inexpensive, and effectual plan to bend the canes to the ground, along the rows, in a mild day of November, being careful not to break the canes. After this, a slight covering of earth from between the rows will hold the canes in place and be a perfect protection from frost. With the aid of the foot to hold the canes down, one man can do the work, but two men will make short work of a large plantation, and the results from this trifling labor are so much more satisfactory, that it should never be neglected. It is not a recommendation that a variety of raspberry is specially hardy, since all are hardy with this slight care, and none are at their best without it. In the spring the earth should be removed from the canes just before the buds start. The canes should then be raised and cut back to three or four feet in height. Thus shortened, many varieties will be sufficiently stocky to be self-supporting. Yet a neater and safer way is to drive stakes in the rows ten feet apart, and then pass two strings of rope yarn, one on either side of the canes and crossing at the stakes, thus giving a loose support on both sides, and confining the branches in the rows. A more careful method is in practice in Europe, to spread and tie the canes in exact position to wires. Except for small lots, this would not be practicable in this country.

The raspberry produces fruit only upon the wood of the previous year. Hence it is necessary, while the old canes are maturing their fruit, to select four or five young shoots in the line of the row for fruiting canes in the following year. All other suckers are to be removed with the hoe, or weeder, as fast as they appear. Early in September the canes which have borne fruit should also be removed, thus giving the entire space to the new canes to gather strength and ripen for the next crop. These canes are to be laid down and covered as before, and cut back in the spring to three or four feet.

The class of raspberries known as Black Caps is generally of stronger growth, and so hardy as not to require winter covering. It will be well for these to increase the distance between the rows to six feet, otherwise the treatment is the same as for the red class.

Summer pinching is recommended by some cultivators and is largely practiced in England.

It consists in nipping the tips of the new shoots when they have attained about three feet in height. The effect is to cause laterals to be thrown out in the form of a little tree. These become the fruiting branches of the following year. In this way the shoot is made stocky and often self-supporting. This is a good way to treat the Black Cap family, since they are hardy and do not require winter covering. But such bushes are manifestly more difficult to lay down and cover, and, more than this, the laterals make a late growth and are very liable to be immature when the frosts overtake them. In the Northern States at least it is better to let the canes grow, and to cut back heroically in the spring. The shoots which start low down on the cane will be most vigorous and the fruit will require less support.

An annual dressing of stable manure will keep a plantation in good heart for a score of years. With this simple, yet systematic care, perhaps more certain, abundant, and satisfactory results are obtained than with any other family fruit. Many new varieties are offered for sale, with high praise. It is best, however, to rely upon those which have been tested, while cautiously trying the novelties in a limited way.

Franconia, Fastolff, Knevett, and Fillbasket

are good old kinds, but seem to be surpassed by Cuthbert and Herstine, which are now deservedly the two favorites. Cuthbert is very productive, large, good, and firm enough to carry to market. Herstine is too melting for the market, but is excellent for family use. Hansell is a new early kind, medium in size and quality, but hardy and very productive. Brinckle's Orange is attractive in color, melting, and excellent in quality, but requires high and careful culture. Perhaps Caroline may take the place of the Orange. Marlboro is an early red, claiming great vigor, productiveness, and other excellences, but it remains to be tested. Of the Black Cap class, Souhegan is early, medium in size, shining black, very productive. Gregg is later, larger, more juicy, and the best of the Caps. Shaffer seems to be a cross between the two classes; is remarkably vigorous, productive; large, juicy fruit, of a dull red color, rather tart, but of rich wild flavor, excellent for preserving.

### THE BLACKBERRY.

The growth of this fruit is so much more gross and thorny than others, that it does not find a welcome in most gardens. It is also liable to injury in winter, and is not easily protected. Very constant, systematic culture will, however, keep the plants within bounds and make them productive. The mode of planting and the treatment is similar to the raspberry, excepting that the distances should be increased to eight feet between the rows. The young shoots should also be summer pruned when about four feet high, which will encourage the throwing out of laterals, which are in turn to be stopped at about eighteen inches in length. Thus a stocky new fruiting bush will be obtained. A strong wire on both sides of the row, fastened to stakes at proper intervals in the row, will keep the plants in place and give sufficient support. Manifestly, it is a difficult process to bend these stiff, thorny plants to the ground and cover them for the winter. Hence it is best to select the kinds which are hardy for each section. Wilson's Early is a noble, large, but rather acid variety, which will endure the winters of the Middle States. Kittatinny is better in quality, but equally tender and more subject to attack of the Flea-louse. For New England and the West, the more hardy kinds, like Snyder, Taylor, Wachusett, and Dorchester, are preferred. Early Harvest is a new kind, said to be hardy, prolific, and very early. Wilson Junior is a new seedling from the old Wilson, which appears to be an improvement in earliness, size, and productiveness. It promises well for the Middle States, but like its parent is probably too tender for higher latitudes.

Root and stem borers affect both the raspberry and blackberry, though not to a serious extent. When the tips of the canes are observed suddenly to droop in June, they should be cut at a little distance below the withered part, to insure the destruction of the egg or larva. Canes that appear to be infested should be cut out in the fall, or spring.

The Bramble Flea-louse (*Psylla rubi*) often infests the foliage of the blackberry, causing great injury in many locations and to some varieties, especially the Kittatinny. Strong tobacco water would probably destroy it, when young. Caterpillars and slugs which feed upon the foliage may be held in check by syringing with hellebore or the other solutions, as may be found necessary. It is the frequent complaint that raspberries do not do as well as formerly. This is doubtless owing, to a considerable extent, to the prevalence of insects. It is earnestly recommended, should the foliage at any time indicate an unhealthy condition, to syringe freely with strong soap-suds, and to follow with tobacco and the kerosene emulsion, if found necessary.

# CHAPTER XIV.

## THE STRAWBERRY.

THIS delicious fruit, the earliest of the season, is so highly appreciated that it is only necessary to dwell upon its mode of culture and the most desirable varieties. The strawberry will grow in a great variety of soils, from warm and light sandy plains, on through rich loams, up to stiff, retentive clay, provided the last has proper drainage. Of course the light soils require most enriching. Some varieties, however, will not thrive in light soils. Richness and depth are most desirable, and the best condition is a rather retentive loam, not subject to drought. The ground should be thoroughly cultivated beforehand, and made fine and friable by frequent harrowing.

As to the amount of fertilizing material there is almost no limit, market gardeners often ploughing in from forty to fifty cords to the acre, before planting. A third part of that amount will, however, give excellent and probably better results.

The beds may be made either in April or in August. There is no doubt that young runners planted as early as August 15th and carefully nursed, not allowing any new runners, will make such strong and fat crowns as will give even larger berries the following June, than can be obtained by any other plan. The yield of the field will not be so great as if planted in the previous spring. But the young plants have the advantage of freshly ploughed ground and fresh fertilizing, at the season of most active growth; they are not weakened by making offsets, but develop to the utmost, as individual plants. It is, therefore, no surprise that our prize fruit comes from August planting. All this is possible. Yet it remains true that spring is generally regarded as the best time for making new plantations. With less care, the plants are more certain to live; the beds become well filled, and a full crop is obtained in the following season. There are advantages in both plans, and circumstances must determine which shall be followed.

For small garden beds a common practice is to lay out beds four feet wide and plant three rows a foot apart, the two outer rows being six inches from the edge of the bed. The plants may be a foot apart in the rows. Thus a bed 100 feet long would require 300 plants. To facilitate good planting, open a furrow on each line with a hand plough, or hoe, in order that the roots of the plant may be spread out evenly and then pressed down firmly, as in natural growth. It is a wretched practice to dibble the roots into a hole and crowd them together in a bunch, as is common. In such beds, the plants being equi-distant, it will be easy to keep down all weeds and also all runners with the hoe.

Better results will be obtained by not allowing any new plants to form, thus throwing all the strength into the one crown which is to give the fruit. By careful and persistent culture and annual fall surface dressing, beds may be kept under this single crown or stool system for several years. It should be borne in mind, however, that a few kinds do not stool well and are better adapted to the matted bed system, which is the plan most in favor in field culture.

In matted culture the field is divided by the hand plough into rows four feet apart, and the plants inserted in the furrows one foot apart. This work is done in April, and the plants are expected to make runners and cover the field, with the exception of a foot space for paths between the rows. When the ground is sufficiently rich it is completely filled, and enormous crops are obtained the second season. The ob-

jection is that the ground is choked with too
many plants, not allowing room for future development.  A common practice is to abandon this
matted mass and plough it under as soon as
the first crop is taken.  If a permanent bed is
desired, it will be necessary to direct the runners as they form, removing any superfluity, and
allowing plants to form only at intervals of
about a foot.

In sections where snow does not lie continu-
ously during winter, it is essential to give a light
covering of evergreen boughs, leaves, sedge, or
light manure, being careful not to rot the plants
by too heavy dressing.  This will be removed
after severe frosts are past.  After the spring
cleaning of weeds and a very light stirring of
the surface, a mulch of straw or clean litter will
serve to keep down the weeds, to keep the ground
moist, and also to protect the fruit from dirt.
In order to keep a bed in good heart, special
fertilizers may be applied in the spring, before
the second and the third crop; such as wood
ashes, superphosphate, or bone.  But a matted
or weedy bed should be abandoned at once.

The strawberry requires a great amount of
water in order to carry heavy crops to perfection.  So important is this that the pump is said
to be the best fertilizer it can have.  If means

of irrigation are at command, it will be a great advantage to give the beds frequent soakings during the period of developing the fruit.

Nature seems to have designed that the strawberry should to a considerable extent be cross fertilized. Hence the flowers are generally imperfect. The flowers of some varieties have no stamens, or only those which are feebly developed. These are called pistillates. Others again have both stamens and pistils and are called staminate, or hermaphrodite. But it is usual, when both organs are found in the same flower, that the pistils are less in number, or are in an enfeebled state. Nature seems to have discouraged the close fertilization and favored a cross. Formerly pistillate varieties, when planted in proximity to a staminate were regarded as most productive. But by continued selection, hermaphrodites, with sufficient vigor of both organs, are obtained, and the result is that the majority of sorts now planted are of this type.

It is asserted that a pistillate, like the Manchester, *e. g.*, is greatly modified by the character of the male variety by which it is fructified, and that the quantity and quality is much improved by judicious mating. This question and that of close fertilizing are of great interest and will furnish the amateur ample opportunity for experiment.

In no other fruit has the change in varieties been so great as in the strawberry. Of old kinds, Hovey is the only one remaining, and its appearance is now a rare sight. Most varieties seem to deteriorate, or become subject to disease. As difference in soil and climate makes such material differences in results, and as new varieties are constantly coming to the front, it is not possible to give a list that will be permanent.

Sharpless is the most popular variety in all sections, at the present time. It is of largest size, of good quality, productive, hermaphrodite, and has more points of merit than any other kind.

Charles Downing has been popular, as of fair quality, uniform good size, and very productive. Of late it has shown a tendency to leaf blight, and it will probably give place to Miner's Prolific, which resembles it, but is thought to surpass it.

Crescent and Wilson are the two most popular market kinds, very productive, but acid and too poor for home use. Manchester is a pistillate which yields large crops and large berries when fructified by Sharpless. Bidwell has not sustained its reputation. James Vick sets an enormous number of berries, beyond its power to mature. Whether any mode of treatment can make it yield a crop of average size is yet to be proved. Jersey Queen is a pistillate of great beauty and excellence and very late; moderately productive. Jucunda and Triomphe de Gaud are two older European kinds, which under generous cultivation, in strong soils and with hill culture, give good results. Wilder is a superb fruit, but has many barren plants, and is unproductive. Hervey Davis is excellent in quality and bears well. Belmont is a seedling raised by Warren Heustis which has not yet been disseminated, but has astonished Boston cultivators for the past two seasons by its fine appearance and enormous crops. It remains to be tested in other hands. For the rest, we must depend upon the catalogues, making trial of novelties in very limited quantities.

The white grub of the May Beetle, or dorbug, as also Root and Crown Borers, often work upon old beds and are very destructive. Dusting with air-slacked lime or watering with Parisgreen or hellebore will check them. But in such cases it is generally better to destroy the beds and the insects together. Leaf rollers, cut worms, and other insects which feed upon the foliage may be destroyed by watering with hellebore, or, after the fruit is matured, with Paris-green. Leaf rust is probably caused by fungous growth. Experiments with sulphur are wanting to test its efficacy. It is customary to drop varieties which are most subject to this disease.

The plan of mowing off all the foliage immediately after fruiting, though seemingly so unnatural, is practiced by many of our best cultivators with excellent results. It is claimed that a new, more healthy, and vigorous plant is thus developed. After the fruit has matured the plant is at comparative rest for a time; both the foliage and the roots dry off, to a considerable extent, and trial proves that the removal of most of the foliage causes a new and more vigorous start, and is a positive benefit.

# CHAPTER XV.

## THE MULBERRY.

THE Red Mulberry (*Morus rubra*) is native to this country, being more abundant in the Middle and Western States, and there attaining a height of 60 or 70 feet. More sparingly it is found as far North as the northern extremity of Lake Champlain. It is an ornamental tree, with dark green leaves. The European variety (*Morus nigra*) much resembles the American, but its black fruit is larger and of better quality, being an inch and a half in length, and of rich, sugary flavor. Downing's Everbearing is a seedling from the Chinese silk variety (*M. multicaulis*), not so large, but juicy, sprightly, vinous, and more agreeable. It suffers from the winters in northern sections. Russian varieties, probably seedlings from *M. nigra*, have been brought to this country by the Mennonites and are largely planted in the Western States. As might be expected among seedlings, the fruit varies somewhat in quality. From these it may be hoped that a valuable selection may be made.

## THE FIG.

In all the Southern States this is a hardy and profitable fruit. At the North, it can easily be raised, to a limited extent, by removing the plants, with a ball of earth attached, and plunging them in a cold cellar for the winter. They are also easily cultivated in tubs. The Angelica, Brown Ischia, Brown Turkey, Brunswick, and Early Violet are all prolific and good, and will ripen a crop in August.

## RHUBARB.

In no sense can this be called a fruit, yet being a hardy perennial, differing so widely from common vegetables, and more resembling fruits in its uses, it may with propriety be here described. It succeeds best in a deep, rich, retentive soil. As its quality depends upon rapidity of growth and consequent tenderness of fibre, it is important to trench deeply before planting, and work in a liberal supply of stable manure. Afterwards the plants should receive an annual fall dressing. It is scarcely possible to manure too highly.

The first season after planting, the stalks should not be cut; and only the largest, and to a limit, should be cut the second year. Afterwards, with little care, they will yield a full supply, so long as they are freely enriched. Should it be desirable to make the stalks specially tender and blanched, this may be done by placing a headless barrel over the crowns in April, and allowing the stalks to grow up within the inclosure. New plantations may be made by division of the roots. Myatt's Linnæus is the best variety for family use, being early, tender, and less acid than other kinds. Victoria is larger and more marketable, but coarser and later.

### ASPARAGUS.

This also is a perennial vegetable, but so distinct, hardy, permanent, and valuable as to claim . a place with fruits. It delights in a deep, rich, and moist soil. Before planting, the ground should be trenched or ploughed to the depth of eighteen inches or two feet. Plants one or two years from the seed are to be preferred. These should be planted in a bed of three rows, a foot apart, and the plants at the same distance in the rows. Thus a bed one hundred feet long would require three hundred plants.

It is well to throw out the surface of the bed with a plough or shovel, in order to facilitate an even planting of the roots, bringing the crown down four inches below the surface when fin-

ished.   An annual top dressing of composted
manure will add an inch or two to the depth
each year.   The crowns will thus be about half
a foot below the surface, and will allow the hoe
or a light cultivator to run over and clean the
ground early in the spring.   As the asparagus is
a maritime plant, and delights in a moist soil,
common salt is recommended as an early spring
dressing.   A new bed should be cut very sparingly the second year after planting, and only
moderately the third year.   With good care and
liberal enriching a bed may be continued indefinitely, and prove as rewarding to the family as
any plant in cultivation.

Asparagus is propagated from seed almost
exclusively, and consequently we have as many
varieties as there are seedlings.   But it is true
that seed selected from strong plants and of good
quality will produce characteristic seedlings.   It
is important that raisers of the plants should
select the best quality of seed.   A strain known
as Connover's Colossal has been favorably received for a few years past.   Mr. J. B. Moore,
of Concord, Massachusetts, has exhibited fine
bunches of what he names Moore's Cross-bred.
Whether cross-bred or not, the seed was undoubtedly carefully selected.   Mr. Moore has had remarkable success in cultivating asparagus upon

light, gravelly soil, by the free use of bone and muriate of potash. His experience may compel us to modify all our received opinions in regard to the requirements of this plant.

Certain it is that with these fertilizers alone, if used in liberal quantity, asparagus of superior size and quality can be produced upon the lightest soil.

# CHAPTER XVI.

## PROPAGATING FRUIT TREES.

It is true that trees can be propagated on a large scale, and by nurserymen, more cheaply than in small lots. The processes are simple and the cost is trifling. But a good deal of care is involved in securing all the conditions, simple though they may be. And in the stage of young and tender growth it is essential to success that all the requirements are uniformly secured. Yet they are all natural and involve but little labor, and the various processes are full of interest and satisfaction when the results are successful. And besides, it often happens that particular kinds are desired to be perpetuated or changed. Every amateur should therefore understand the principles, and be able to practice the art of propagating with success.

*From the Seed.* — Apple and pear stocks are raised from seed sown in drills, in rich land, which will give strong growth, fit to be dug at the end of the first season. The seed should be sown thin, so that each plant will have room enough to grow, and should receive a covering of about one inch of earth, which should be pressed firmly upon the seed. Mazzard and Mahaleb, cherry and plum stones, should be kept in moist sand through the fall and winter, in boxes which should be allowed to freeze and be kept in this state, or as cold as possible, until spring. After this they should be planted as apple and pear seeds.

Peach stones are wintered in wet sand, in boxes in the open air, allowing them to freeze and thaw frequently. By this process the stones either will open of themselves or may be easily cracked with a nut cracker. The seed should then be planted in furrows, made with a plough, three feet apart, and the stones or meat four inches apart in the row. Wood ashes strewed in the furrow and mixed with a hoe will prove an excellent fertilizer for the peach. If the stones have been well preserved and cracked with care the growth will be uniform, and the stocks in good condition to bud in August following.

All other fruit seedlings should be dug from their beds in late autumn, and heeled in thickly and to a good depth in cold frames, receiving a moderate degree of frost. If the apple stocks are wanted for winter grafting (a process which will be hereafter described), they should be so covered as to be accessible.

In early spring, the stocks which are intended for budding should have their tap roots shortened by a clean cut of the knife. If free from small fibrous roots, which are worse than useless, it will be well to dip the roots in a thin wash of clay and cow dung, thus insuring them against drying. It is well to dip all trees in such a wash, when removed, provided the fibres are not left wadded together to cause decay. It is the approved practice to plant fruit stocks in rows three and a half feet apart, and one foot in the row. After thorough ploughing, a line is stretched, and a trench is cut with a spade, deep enough to receive the stocks on the same level as the growth of the previous year. One boy holds the stock at the right distance, and a man standing off on the opened side of the line, with a hoe bottom-side up, presses a little fine earth *very* firmly against the stock, bringing it to a plump upright position. The trench is then to be filled, and if the stocks are not so firm in the ground that they will not yield to a slight pull, a gentle pressure of the foot on both sides of the row is advisable. Loose planting is the cause of many failures. If rightly planted, in rich soil, they will make vigorous growth, and be in good **condition** for budding in midsummer.

**There** are five methods of perpetuating desirable varieties of fruits and other plants, which will here be described.

*By Division.* — Many plants, like the Japan Quince, **throw** offsets which may be separated from the parent and form new plants. Others, like the raspberry and blackberry, send up numerous suckers from the root. The strawberry, on the contrary, sends out runners on the surface **which take root. This is** Nature's work, with little **for the cultivator to** do, but to avail himself of the results.

*By Cuttings.* — Next to division, this is the simplest and cheapest process, when it can readily be applied. The currant, gooseberry, grape, and quince, as well as many trees and shrubs, like the Willow, Poplar, Spiræas, and Weigelias, will root with facility from hard wood cuttings. Indeed, nearly all kinds of wood may be induced to emit roots by a slow process of softening the wood, under favorable conditions of heat and moisture. Partially ripened wood, usually called soft wood cuttings, will root quicker than harder wood, provided a little foliage is left, which is sustained in a cool, moist atmosphere until the roots form. This is the ordinary way of striking roses and shrubs in shaded frames, in the months of July and August, the surface soil being pure fine sand, as a guard against damping. Such cold frames require to be opened and closed, in order to maintain an even temperature, and also a careful supply of water, as needed. But for fruits, ripened wood is preferable. Still it is better to take this wood before it becomes too hard, and especially before it is dried by the frosts. Cuttings taken in early September and buried in a horizontal position in a warm and moderately moist soil will be rooted at the end of autumn. But the objection is that the tops will also start and perish upon exposure. The safest course is to take the cuttings about the time of the first sharp frosts and heel them in, very thickly, in beds of light, sandy loam, using only enough soil to separate the cuttings. The beds may be three feet wide and as long as is needed. A bed six feet long would hold many thousand cuttings. The tops should remain exposed to the frosts, and as the earth is warmer than the air during the fall months, considerable progress in callousing will be obtained, and at the same time the tops will be kept dormant. Just before the ground closes the bed should be rounded up with earth, covering the tops entirely. Shutters may then be placed over the

bed to protect from rain. Early in the spring
the bed should be uncovered and the earth removed from the tops, and as soon as the ground
is dry the cuttings should be lifted and planted as
directed for stocks, but in rows eighteen inches
apart, if cultivated by hand. Currants and
quinces may be from four to six inches in the
rows, but grapes will require more distance.
The usual length of cuttings is about nine inches,
and they should be selected from strong, mature
growth of the same season. As the tissues just
under a bud are favorable for granulation and
the formation of roots, it is best to make the
lower cut near the base of an eye. The upper
eyes should not project more than two or three
inches above the surface. Grape vines and
many other hard wood plants may be raised
from cuttings with a single eye, but since there
is little wood
left to sustain
the eye, in such
a case, the aid

Fig. 15.

of bottom heat
will be required.
In a propagating
bed of sand over
waterpipes, these

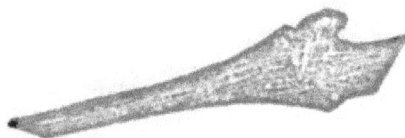

Fig. 16.

eyes root with facility. Before the roots interlace, they should be potted, and early in June, when well established, they may be planted in rich, mellow, open ground. The different forms of single eye cuttings of the grape may be seen

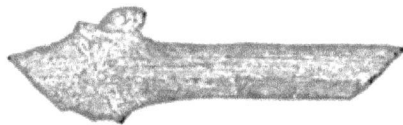

Fig. 17.

in Figs. 15, 16, and 17. As the deposit of cambium is known to be greater near the base of an eye, the theory for Fig. 17 was that roots would form more readily at the eye, while the wood projecting above would retain some sap to sustain the eye. In practice probably it does more harm than good, by increasing the liability of displacement. Fig. 16 shows the lower and under part of the cutting shaved off, in order to expose more surface for the formation of roots. Practically, the surface is in danger of absorbing too much moisture. Fig. 15 shows the best form, the least amount of surface to be calloused, while the roots will freely form from under the bark as well as at the cut. The cost of raising cuttings in quantity is very trifling.

*By Layers.* — A layer is but a modified form of a cutting, with this advantage, that the cutting is not separated from the parent plant, but still draws its support from it until new roots are formed. In the case of many vines, like the

honeysuckles, roots are formed in abundance
when the branches are left simply to trail upon
the surface of the ground. In other cases it is
only necessary to bend the branches into trenches
and throw a little covering of soil upon them in
order to get well rooted plants. But with the
majority of plants, includ-
ing the quince and the
grape, a little assistance
with the knife is required.
An incision of any kind
will tend to arrest the descending flow of sap and
induce the formation of roots. A simple tongue

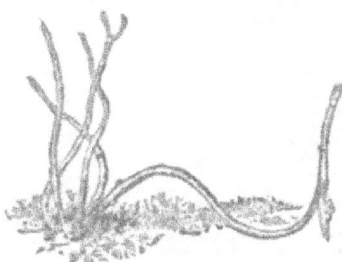

Fig. 18.

passing under an eye, as in Fig. 18, is all that is
required, where the branches are sufficiently flexi-
ble. But it often happens that, when the cut is
thus made, the shoot is greatly weakened, if not
broken entirely off, in bringing it to an upright
position. A safer mode and one which brings
the tongue into a better position for throwing out
roots is to make the incision on the top of the
bending branch, and then to turn the tongue to
one side of the branch, as seen in Fig. 19. The
liability to break is much lessened, and roots will
strike out in a more natural direction. Layers are
more generally made from half-ripened wood,
in July and early August, and there is no doubt

that roots will form more rapidly at this season
than in the spring. But the young roots do not
always become sufficiently strong in the brief time
before frosts, and the layers may require another
season before the new plant is fit to be separated

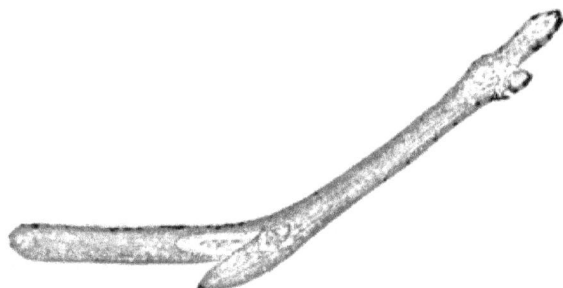

Fig 19.

from its parent. This often happens when a
drought occurs in the latter part of the season.
For this and other reasons, layering may be done
before growth starts in the spring. In the case
of grapes, the form of growth may be regulated
in the preceding season by leading out several
horizontal shoots and stopping the tips when six
or eight feet long, thus causing a great number
of laterals to develop, all of which will make excellent plants by fall. Fig. 20 illustrates the
rapidity with which vines may be thus increased.
Strong pegs will be required to hold stiff branches
firmly in position. A handful of fine leaf mould
and sand at the tongue will greatly assist in
developing roots. Sufficient covering of soil and

a light mulch should be given to prevent drying.
Layers will usually winter best as attached to
the stools, being well banked up or mulched
with leaves and evergreen boughs to protect

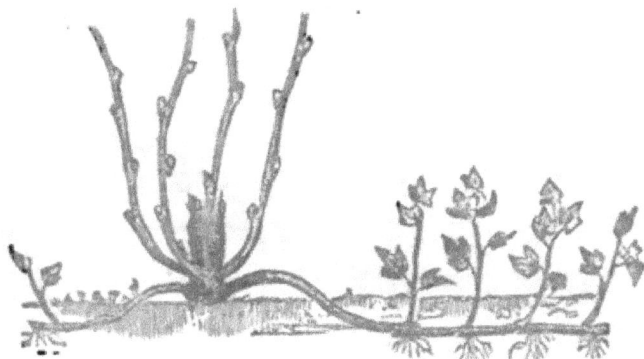

Fig. 20.

from "heaving." In early spring all well-rooted
plants should be separated and planted in rows;
thus making room for a subsequent crop.

*By Budding.* — At periods of active flow of
sap the bark of trees will readily separate from
the wood. When this can be done, buds may be
inserted under the bark and upon the sap wood,
which will unite with the tree and yet preserve
their identity and characteristics. Thus a tiny
bud of a sweet apple, though inserted on the
stock of the sourest crab, and drawing all its
nourishment from it, will yet be true to its origin
and yield fruit after its kind. This operation
may be performed at any time when the bark
lifts freely, provided buds sufficiently mature

can be obtained. But the time of most certain success is when the summer growth is about to cease and the flow of sap will be less abundant. Both the buds and the sap will then be in best condition for a speedy union. Upon cutting the scion from which the buds are to be taken, the leaves should at once be cut, leaving about a quarter of an inch of the foot stalk of the leaf, which will be long enough to hold the bud. After the foliage is removed these scions may be kept several days without injury, if wrapped in damp cloth, or in moss.

The different steps in the process of budding may be seen in the figures. With a keen, thin blade the bud is cut from the scion, as seen in Fig. 21. The length of the cut varies, but in general is about half an inch above the bud, and slightly longer below.

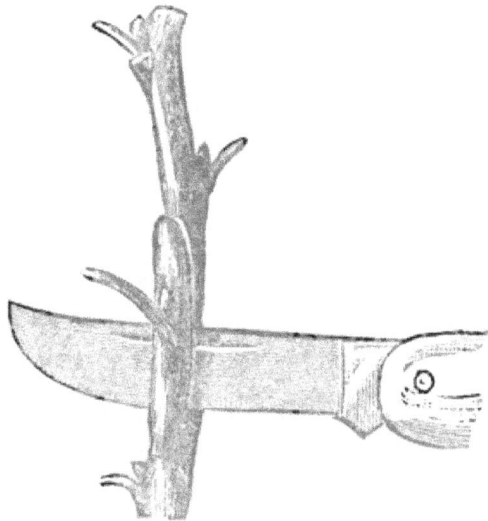

Fig. 21.

As little wood as is possible should be cut with the bud, and when it does not adhere firmly it may be re-

moved. But there is danger of injury to the
bud, if this is done unskillfully. Fig. 22 shows
the perpendicular and horizontal slits through
the bark of the stock, and Fig. 23 shows

Fig. 22.    Fig. 23.    Fig. 24.    Fig. 25.

the lips of the bark slightly raised by the thin
hilt of the budding knife. In Fig. 24 the bud
is seen slipped into its place, the bark lapping
smoothly over it. It is now necessary to bind
the bud so firmly that the air and rain will be
excluded, as may be seen in Fig. 25. The soft
and moistened strings selected from bass mats
have been used for this purpose. A grass called
Roffea is coming into use as an excellent material
for tying. It is very soft, pliable, and strong,
and is a decided improvement on bass bark, or

mat strings. It may be obtained at trifling cost at the seed stores. If prepared with a very slight coating of wax, the work will be more easily and better done. Some varieties of trees have an excessive flow of sap, and the buds are liable to be "drowned out," as it is termed. In such cases it is recommended by some to make the horizontal slit at the bottom of the perpendicular incision, and then to insert the bud upwards instead of slipping it down as before. This latter method, namely, of inverting the cross (thus, $\perp$), is that which is practiced with maples and other ornamental trees, but is not required for fruits. Other forms have also been suggested, but they are rather ingenious than useful. The common cross, $\top$, will be found sufficient for all ordinary cases.

The conditions of success are: vigorous stocks which peel freely; sufficiently mature buds; a smooth, thin cut of the bud, with but little wood adhering; no roughing of the cambium under the bark; a good fit of the bud; without delay; and an even binding of the bark so as to exclude all air. In about ten days or a fortnight after this work is done, if the stocks are vigorous, the strings will begin to bind, when they will require to be loosened, or, if the union appears to be secure, a drawn cut with a sharp knife, on the opposite side of the **stock from** the bud, will give permanent relief. **In the** early spring the stock **is cut** away a few inches above the bud, and this projecting stem may serve as a support **to which** the young shoot may be tied, **if necessary. In July the** shoot will be strong enough **for self-support,** and the stub **should be** cut away close down to the bud, so that the wound may close over. Budding is the method by which the great majority of fruit trees are propagated in the nurseries. **The union of the** bud with the young **stock is smooth; the work** is done at a season **of the year when work** is not pressing; and **the** labor involved is less than that of **grafting.** More careful after watching is necessary, in relieving the ties and in training the **buds,** and cutting away the stubs. **The work is** rapidly performed, from five hundred **to one** thousand buds being an easy day's **work for a** man and a **boy. Pear** stocks are liable to leaf-blight early in August, **and** therefore require to be budded before growth stops. Peaches, on the other hand, are **in active** growth into September, and work **upon them may be delayed** well **into** August.

*By Grafting.* — **This may be** considered but a modification of the method by budding, the scion being of greater length than the bud, and inserted upon the stock at another period of growth, and in different ways. It may also be regarded as but a modified form of a cutting, inserted upon a stock already provided with roots, instead of inserting into the soil, for the formation of its own roots. Having strong and vigorous stocks it is obvious that speedy results would follow the engrafting of scions. The usual time for the operation is early spring, when both stock and scion are dormant, but about ready to start. Plums and cherries require to be grafted very early, before there are signs of any flow of sap, or swelling of the bud. But provided the scions be kept dormant, apples, pears, and grapes may be grafted much later, even until in full leaf. In a close house, or frame, with moist heat, grafting may be success-fully performed at any season and with partially ripened wood, but in the open air it is necessary that the scion, at least, should be in a dormant condition. There are three conditions essential to successful union, viz.: First, that the inner bark and cambium of the stock and scion come in contact and coincide with each other to some extent; second, that this union be secured by a firm pressure; third, that a permanent covering be applied which shall exclude air and moisture. Numerous modes of accomplishing these ends have been devised, all of which may be resolved into modifications of three forms, namely, cleft, whip, and saddle grafting.

Cleft grafting is the method usually applied to large trees, and wherever the stocks are much larger than the scions. The trunk or limbs of the stock are usually sawed and smoothed off with a square cut. With a splitting-iron, as seen in Fig. 26, a split is made, usually down the centre of the limb, as shown in Fig. 27. The split is to be opened by the wedges at either end of the

Fig. 26.

splitting iron. The scion is then to be cut in a wedge form corresponding to the split in the stock. The side of the scion which is to be within the stock should be shaved slightly thinner than the outer edge, in order that the pressure of the stock may be firm at the bark. As the bark of the stock is usually thicker than the new bark of the scion, it is necessary in such a case to place the scion slightly within the outer bark, making sure, by careful inspection, that the

Fig. 27.

inner bark and cambium of stock and scion
shall coincide. Fig. 28 shows the scion inserted.
A bud is usually selected to be at the level
of the stock, which will be protected by the
covering, and may prove to be the best eye for
the future shoot. Generally but one bud above
this is left on the scion. If
the stock is an inch or more
in diameter, the scion will usually be held sufficiently firm,
after the withdrawal of the
wedge. Should this prove not
to be the case, a ligature will
be necessary to draw the two
sides firmly to the scion. But
this involves the removal of
the ligature soon after growth

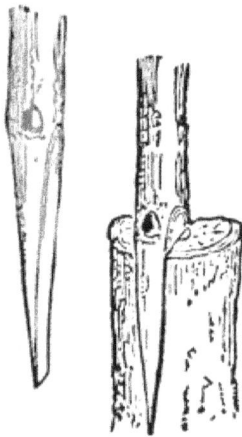

Fig. 28.

commences, and as this is objectionable, it is
better to adopt another mode of grafting small
stocks.

The exposed parts and the upper end of the
scion, if cut, should immediately be covered with
some material impervious to air and rain. Clay
worked up with cow dung and hair has been
used as a natural and healing plaster. But the
application is not easy or agreeable, and worst
of all, there is liability to cracking and crum-
bling. Grafting wax is more permanent and is

applied with more rapidity. The common formula for making this is to melt together three
parts rosin, three parts pure beeswax, two parts
beef tallow. After melting and when partially
cooled, pull *ad libitum*, to toughen. Linseed
oil is a vegetable product, and perhaps preferable to tallow. A cheaper, harder, and better
composition may be made of four parts rosin,
one part beeswax, and one part linseed oil.
Should this prove too hard in cold weather,
more oil may be added. A very hard wax is
used in the French
nurseries, with best
results. The wax
may be heated in a
skillet and applied
with a b r u s h, or
w h e n warmed in
water may be spread
by hand. It is im-
portant that every
exposed part, as well
as the cut at the end
of the scion, should
be covered with the
wax. Thus protected

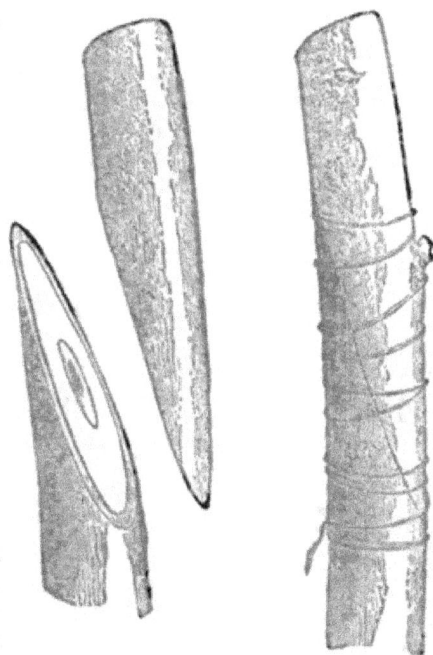

Fig 29.

there is little more care, except to watch and
protect the future shoot and remove suckers.

Whip grafting is the method more commonly applied when the stock and the scion are about of the same size, although it is not limited to this condition. Fig. 29 indicates how perfectly the stock and scion may be made to correspond. This is the simplest form. But in the case of wood that is not brittle, it is safer to slit a tongue in the stock and a corresponding one in the scion, as seen in Fig. 30. A little practice will soon enable a good knifesman to make a close adjustment of the parts. But it is not to be expected that the scion will exactly cover the entire cut surface of the stock. It is only necessary that the union of cambium should be perfect at some point, though the more entire this union is, the more certain will be the success. The scions are secured to the stock by a bandage of waxed cloth, drawn sufficiently tight to hold the scion firmly, and to exclude the air. The cloth is made

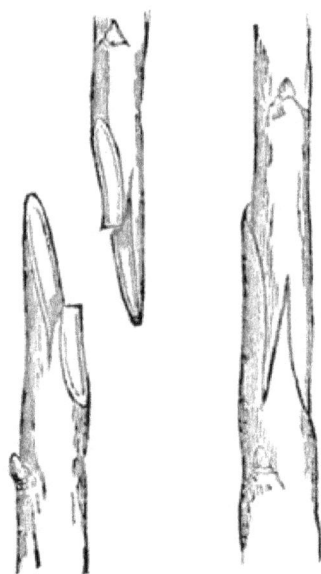

Fig. 30.

by dipping strips of thin cotton cloth about four inches wide into hot wax, and then drawing them under the edge of a pane of glass used as a scraper. This gives a smooth, thin waxed-cloth with just enough wax to adhere when slightly warmed, strong enough to bind to a close union, and yet weak enough to yield to increased growth. These strips are again cut into narrow strips about three eighths of an inch wide, and into lengths sufficient to wind smoothly and completely cover the work.

Whip grafting is the method by which nurserymen propagate apples and many other plants, in cellars, in the winter time. The stocks are stored where accessible, and the work progresses throughout the winter. Instead of cloth a prepared waxed paper is found to be sufficiently strong, and more ready to yield to growth. The Roffea grass may also prove to be a good tying material. Apple grafts are packed in boxes, in sawdust, or some other retentive non-conductor, and stored away in cold cellars, until planting time. Various modifications of whip grafting are practiced, the most common being a side insertion, as seen in Fig. 31. This is a good form for grafting the

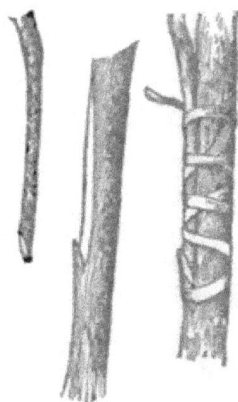

Fig. 31.

rose, which being brittle in its wood does not readily take a tongue. The scion is, however, held securely in its place by the notch in the stock, and a good eye and hand will make the cuts so that the bark will coincide over most of the surface. When this work is done in a greenhouse, a little sphagnum moss is tied around the scion and stock to preserve a moist condition. In this way evergreen trees and a great variety of stocks, which are comparatively difficult to graft, are treated very successfully. In the close, even temperature and humidity of a glass case within the greenhouse, a careful gardener will succeed in grafting almost every plant with its allied stock. In all cases he endeavors to have the sap of the stock in motion and slightly in advance of the scion.

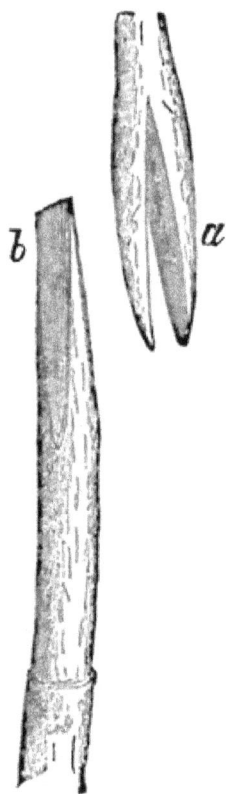

Saddle grafting can scarcely be called more than a modified form of whip grafting.

Here the stock is sloped off on each side, as seen in Fig. 32 *b*, while the scion *a* is slit so as to cover the stock. In Fig. 33 the work is seen before the bandage is applied, and shows how smooth will be the after growth, if success-

Fig. 32.

ful. Scions may be kept dormant until late in the spring, by packing in a refrigerator or ice-house. They then may be shaved to a point on one side and inserted under the bark of the stock, which will separate from the wood after growth has commenced. Fig. 34 illustrates this form, which is a modification of whip and of saddle grafting, and also of budding. Scions should be cut in the fall or early winter, before the wood is any way injured or pinched by frosts. They should be kept in a cold place, in slightly moist earth, where the wood

Fig. 33.

will be preserved in a plumb dormant condition. After grafting little care is required, save to remove any sprouts or suckers which may start, and to loosen any ligatures which may cut into the wood.

There is a prevalent opinion that grafting is a difficult art, and that only knifesmen of exceptional skill and experience can succeed. But this is a mistaken notion; the conditions are simple and the process is simple.

Fig. 34.

With a careful observance of the rules, and after a little practice, any amateur should become an expert, and take great delight in experiments in this direction.

It is no small part of the reward in fruit culture that ways for experiment and study are opened in all directions, and that Nature seems kindly to encourage every attempt to understand her laws.

# INDEX.